Truth or Territory:

A Biblical Approach to Spiritual Warfare

Jim Osman

Foreword by Justin Peters

This book is self-published by James C. Osman II and Kootenai Community Church Publishing.

Text copyright © 2015 James Clancy Osman II

Cover artwork provided by Josh Comstock from http://www.PeaceHarbor.co.

Website hosting provided by Thomas Leo from http://www.TLCWebHosting.com.

http://www.TruthOrTerritory.com

http://www.KootenaiChurch.org

Dedication

This book is dedicated to the loving, joy-filled, faithful saints that gather as Kootenai Community Church who make it a joy to serve as an undershepherd of Jesus Christ.

Why This Book? - A Personal Note

Thank you for purchasing this book!

There may be a number of reasons why you purchased this book. There are a number of reasons why I wrote it.

First, I wrote the content of this book as a series of articles published in our church newsletter over the course of a year and a half. I have been asked numerous times about some of the doctrines and practices mentioned in these pages. I decided to put the answers down in writing so I might have a resource to hand to those who ask in the future. It is my earnest desire that God may use His truth in these pages to purify His church, reform His church, and equip the saints for the work of ministry.

Second, having written the material, I desired to make this available to an audience beyond the walls of my own church family. Initially I did this by making the articles available on our website (www.kootenaichurch.org) for free. Putting this material in a book format makes it even more accessible to an even larger audience. It is still my desire that God may use this for His glory in equipping His people.

Third, I have decided to make this material available for purchase in both print and electronic format as a fundraiser for Kootenai Community Church's new church building. We are in the process - and have been since 2002 - of building a new church facility for our church family. We have committed ourselves to doing this without taking out a loan and to only build as we can pay for it. Consequently, it has been a long process, and the Body of Christ at Kootenai has been amazingly patient and adaptable through it all.

We have been meeting in a school cafeteria for 13 years (as of 2015). This has involved unloading and setting up and then putting away chairs, sound system, and music equipment week after week for that whole time. Being in a rented facility has imposed many limitations on our ministry and yet folks have adapted. We are thankful that God has provided a meeting place for us for these years, but we are looking forward to getting in our own building with all the opportunities that that will bring.

All of the proceeds from the sale of this book go directly to Kootenai Community Church for the purpose of completing our church building. Thank you for your contribution to that end!

Soli Deo Gloria!

Update 2018: I am pleased to report that Kootenai Community Church moved into its new church building June 1, 2018. After 16 years of meeting in an elementary school cafeteria while building a new facility, we joyfully moved in with no debt! We thank God for His gracious and faithful provision through His people!

Other Books by Jim Osman

Selling the Stairway to Heaven: Critiquing the Claims of Heaven Tourists

The Prosperity of the Wicked: A Study of Psalm 73

God Doesn't Whisper
Available in 2019

Contents

Foreword   xiii
Acknowledgments   xvii
Preface   xxi

Introduction   1

Part 1: Establishing Biblical Principles
Chapter 1 - Our Source of Intelligence   11
Chapter 2 - Truth or Territory?   21
Chapter 3 - The Enemy and His Army   35
Chapter 4 - The World and the Flesh   47

Part 2: Exposing Unbiblical Practices
Chapter 5 - Carnal Weapons: Hedges   61
Chapter 6 - Carnal Weapons: Hexes   75
Chapter 7 - Carnal Weapons: Binding Satan   89
Chapter 8 - Carnal Weapons: Rebuking Satan   101
Chapter 9 - Carnal Weapons: Spiritual Mapping   115

Part 3: Explaining Biblical Perspectives
Chapter 10 - Can a Christian Be Demon-Possessed?   129
Chapter 11 - Is Christ's Authority Ours?   147
Chapter 12 - What about Exorcisms?   161
Chapter 13 - Spiritual Warfare and Sanctification   175

Part 4: Examining a Biblical Passage
Chapter 14 - The Posture of a Soldier   191
Chapter 15 - The Protection for a Soldier 207

Chapter 16 - Conclusion: A Final Appeal   223

About the Author   227

Foreword

There exists a great and tragic paradox among most of professing Christendom. We live in a day and age of unparalleled access to almost unlimited biblical resources. Christian bookstore shelves are filled with works from a dizzying array of authors on an equally dizzying array of subjects. Christian conferences promising to equip people to have success and victory in every area of life are filled to capacity. The advent of the internet age has made almost every sermon from almost every preacher, both living and dead, available at the click of a mouse.

And yet, with all of this ease of access to biblical information, never have both society at large and the church itself been more ignorant of biblical doctrine. All studies done on the subject confirm that people have but a cursory knowledge of the Bible – at best. Rare are those who are willing to follow the Apostle Paul's directive to "study to show themselves approved unto God" (2 Timothy 2:15). Most are content with getting their theology from sound bites and sermonettes which have little, if any, grounding in Scripture.

Few areas of the Christian life are more misunderstood than that of spiritual warfare. The topic of spiritual warfare is a popular one. With its images of angels and demons brandishing swords in unseen battles and the assumption that we are to engage in such battles or fail to do so at our own peril, spiritual warfare generates tremendous interest. Books and conferences on the subject provide instructions on how to wage this warfare by breaking generational curses, praying hedges of protection, exorcisms, mapping the spiritual realm, rebuking and binding the demonic hierarchy all the way up to Satan himself. If these instructions are meticulously followed, we are told, victory is assured – at least until the next frightful encounter.

Such practices used to be confined to the Catholic and charismatic churches. Not anymore. Today these techniques are almost universally accepted (and universally misunderstood) among the evangelical world. People assume that these prescribed machinations are indispensable tools for living a materially and spiritually victorious life.

Would it surprise you to learn that none of these techniques is necessary or even biblical?

Spiritual warfare is real, to be sure. The Bible has much to say about it. The problem, though, is that almost all contemporary teaching on this subject is decidedly unbiblical. Popular teachers have wrested certain Scriptures out of their biblical contexts and have fabricated a theology that is successful in selling books and filling conferences, but utterly useless in equipping the Christian for the true battles which await him.

The Apostle Paul instructed his readers in Corinth "not to exceed what is written" (1 Corinthians 4:6). In other words, in both our doctrine and practice we are not to exceed the parameters given to us and preserved for us by God in His Word. When biblical parameters are exceeded, God's protection is abandoned. The tragic irony is that contemporary teaching on spiritual warfare is actually exposing the undiscerning masses to the very demonic deception from which it alleges to protect!

In *Truth Or Territory*, Jim Osman has done the church a great service. He takes the confusing theological cauldron brewed by modern spiritual warfare "experts" and shatters it against God's Word. With precision and clarity he demonstrates that true spiritual warfare is not a war fought with mantras and incantations but rather with biblical truth.

Truth Or Territory will be of great benefit to the professor, pastor, and layman alike. A work like this is sorely needed in the body of Christ today and it is my prayer that your obedient walk with our King will be both enriched and simplified by its reading. Jim is a personal friend of mine and one for whom I have the utmost respect as a pastor, theologian, husband, father, and disciple of our Lord. I commend this resource to you with great joy and enthusiasm.

In His Service,

Justin Peters
justinpeters.org

Acknowledgments

The challenge of writing acknowledgments for a book lies in trying to decide in what order to include the many people who are most certainly worthy of acknowledgment. Should people be included in order of chronology, contribution, or closeness to the author?

If I begin chronologically, then I have to start with my Fourth Year Bible Professor, Phil Powers. Phil would be surprised to learn that he is mentioned here but not nearly as surprised as to hear that I actually wrote a book and asked people to purchase it. Phil was instrumentally used by God to challenge my thinking on theologies and issues raised in this book. I sat under Phil's invaluable tutelage during my fourth year at Millar College of the Bible in Pambrun, Saskatchewan. Thanks to Phil, I was required to buy *A Holy Rebellion*, a work you will find quoted throughout the pages of this book. Thanks, Phil.

If I begin with those who have contributed to this work then I have to first mention my good friend and mentor Brian Atmore, once President of Millar College of the Bible, and then pastor at Creston Baptist Church. Brian's contribution to my life, ministry, and preaching has been, and continues to be, immeasurable. He pored over the manuscript for this book with a red pen in hand and provided pages of hand-written, substantial insights and editorial suggestions. Brian's careful eye and ear for the written word are rare and valuable gifts. I am sure he used up half a dozen red pens, but he has made this book better in every way. Brian, all the triplets in these acknowledgments are in your honor. Thanks!

Brian is not the only one who has had a hand in this book. There are a number of people who have made contributions. Thomas Leo designed the original cover and Josh Comstock the updated one. Jenny Leo provided valuable editing and feedback during the writing process. My secretary, Marcia Whetsel, helps each week to free up some time that I can devote to writing.

Jason Upchurch, pastor at Redeemer Bible Church in Deer Park, Washington provided valuable encouragement and commentary related to my tone. Many sentences in this book sounded much harsher, shriller, and more offensive than they do now. I have Jason to thank for any gracious tone present in these pages. Anything sounding intentionally offensive that remains in these pages is an oversight. I intend to be thought-provoking and not abrasive. I trust that Jason has helped me strike that balance. Thanks, Jason.

I am grateful for the thoughtful input, encouragement, and kind words of Justin Peters (justinpeters.org) who was gracious enough to write the foreword to this book. Justin's support for and continued promotion of this book have served as a powerful impetus for its completion. Thanks, Justin.

Or should I begin with those closest to me? If so, then I must begin by thanking God for my lovely wife who is the greatest blessing in my life apart from salvation in Jesus Christ. Her friendship and love are more valuable to me than life itself. The time she has spent in proofreading this work, not once, but twice, she can never get back. She did it without a word of complaint. She has a careful eye for typos without which, this book would not be worth the paper it is printed on. Thankfully this was a labor of love for her, at least I hope so. Maybe she just didn't want people to think she married an idiot!

I am also unspeakably grateful for the Body of faithful, loving, serving believers that I have the joy of being a part of each Lord's Day. The believers at Kootenai Community Church have read these chapters in the form of articles in our church newsletter and provided valuable input and encouragement. It is a joy to serve the Lord with them and grow together in the Word of God. They are my joy and crown (1 Thessalonians 2:19-20). The elders of the flock that I serve with at Kootenai, Dave Rich, Jess Whetsel, and Cornel Rasor, are among my closest friends and among the most trustworthy, honorable, and gifted men I have ever had the pleasure of knowing.

It is a gift of grace to be yoked together with them in the work of shepherding.

I am almost certain I have missed someone. As the Athenians had an altar to the Unknown God (Acts 17:23), I offer my sincere thanks to you, the "Unknown Contributor" and helper in this work. Thanks! Without you, this book would not exist - I think.

I leave the most significant for last. I thank My God and Father of the Lord Jesus Christ for His inexpressible gift - salvation in His Son. I thank Him for choosing me for salvation and drawing me to Himself. I thank Him for giving me the gifts of repentance and faith in July of 1987 when I first believed unto eternal life. It amazes me daily that God has saved a wretch such as I.

Thank You, O Gracious God for saving me, sanctifying me, and securing me in Your Son. In Christ, I know I will be presented blameless before Your throne with exceeding joy to Your own eternal glory!

To God alone be glory, praise, and honor both now and in eternity! Amen.

Preface

The book you are about to read began as a series of articles published in the monthly newsletter of the church I pastor in Kootenai, Idaho. I originally planned a nine-part series that grew to sixteen. I intended to provide written answers to some oft-asked questions concerning practices among Christians in the area of spiritual warfare.

There is great need for clear, biblical thinking on this subject. A few reliable books exist on the subject of spiritual warfare, many of which you will see quoted and referenced in the pages that follow. They are rare and are quickly lost in the tempestuous sea of bad teaching.

I am under no delusions of grandeur which might cause me to believe that I can write a definitive work on the subject. I stand on the shoulders of the giants of the faith who have gone before. My sincere hope and prayer is that Jesus Christ, our great King, might use this work to liberate His people from superstition and empower them to fight the war for truth - biblically.

In Chapters 1 and 2 we examine the foundational issues of the sufficiency of Scripture and the nature of the spiritual battle. In Chapters 3 and 4 we take a look at what the Bible says regarding the three enemies that a Christian faces, namely, the world, the flesh, and the devil. Five chapters (5-9), address wrong warfare practices prevalent in many Christian circles. I will explain these practices, give examples of their use, and examine the texts commonly cited for support. In Chapters 10-12 we tackle some key questions: Can a Christian be demon possessed? Is Christ's authority my authority? and, What about exorcisms? In Chapter 13 we examine the connection between spiritual warfare and sanctification. Finally, in

Chapters 14-15 we study Ephesians 6, the well-known armor of God section, in the light of its context.

May our gracious, sovereign, triune God use this book to equip the saints, refute those who contradict, defend the once-and-for-all delivered faith, contend for the truth, advance His Word and glorify His most holy name!

Let us test all things and hold fast to that which is true!

Soli Deo Gloria!

Jim Osman
Pastor/Teacher
Kootenai Community Church

An Introduction

There are few topics in Christianity that are as clouded by misunderstanding, false assumptions, bad information, unbiblical practices, and mystical, superstitious, beliefs as the subject of spiritual warfare. Consequently, the subject creates some passionate and oftentimes heated responses from people who have invested in certain practices, techniques, or modern conventions.

While preaching through Ephesians 6 during the worship services of the church I pastor, I took four weeks in the middle of the chapter to present what the Bible says concerning spiritual warfare from various passages of Scripture. During one message titled, "Wrong Warfare," I quoted from popular author, Neil T. Anderson, as an illustration of a wrong approach to certain aspects of spiritual warfare. After the sermon, a lady visiting our church went up to another lady who was a member and said with all seriousness, "You need to get out of this church! This man is a heretic! He is teaching heresy!" This visitor was heavily invested in the writings and teachings of Neil T. Anderson and my critique of some of his teachings made me a "heretic" in her book. Obviously, this is a very controversial and heated subject in some circles.

Spiritual warfare is a very popular topic. A quick search on Amazon's website for "Spiritual Warfare" yielded over 2,700 products. If you think that is a lot to digest, don't bother googling the words and trying to sort through all that the internet has to offer.[1]

Where can a person, hungry to learn about the spiritual conflict in which we are involved, turn to find answers? Searching for books on the subject is likely to lead you into a swamp of very confusing waters. You are just as likely to pick up the unbiblical teachings of Neil T. Anderson[2] as you are to purchase something much more

---

[1] Google results for "Spiritual Warfare" yielded 6,310,000 results.

[2] *Winning Spiritual Warfare* by Neil T. Anderson came in at number nine in an Amazon.com search.

biblical by Charles Spurgeon.[3] You will find a dozen different approaches to spiritual warfare from hundreds of different authors.

There is an ever present hunger for teaching on this subject. Christians, young and old, new and seasoned, want to know about angels and demons. They want to know about the spiritual struggle in the heavens that Scripture describes. That ever-present hunger is met by a never-ending stream of books and teachings which promise deliverance from demons, victory over sin, and triumph in the spiritual battle.

As I will show in the pages to come, much of what is taught in Christian circles concerning spiritual warfare is not found in Scripture at all. Much of it is pagan, superstitious nonsense. Much of it consists of patently unbiblical techniques which rely upon Scriptures taken out of their contexts and twisted. Some of it is pure tradition - things we have been taught or heard preached - which have never been tested by Scripture.

Error is rampant in this realm and I don't think it is by accident. I believe the enemy of our souls would love to get us off track, trip us up, or distract us with methodologies that are unbiblical, unprofitable, and unproductive. If Satan can mislead a Christian concerning true biblical spiritual warfare, he can neutralize that Christian's effectiveness, and in effect, keep him out of the battle entirely.

This is a subject where Satan has a vested interest in confusing, misleading, and deceiving God's people. Consequently, this is a subject where discernment and clear biblical thinking is desperately needed.

The approach that people take toward this subject runs the gamut from denial to delusion, from apathy to zeal. Some people deny that Satan exists, others see a demon behind every bush and under every stone. Some folks don't give a passing thought to Satan, his activity, or his ploys. Others are so preoccupied with the demonic that they hardly have time for anything other than battling demons,

---

[3] I highly recommend *Spiritual Warfare in a Believer's Life*, a collection of sermons by Charles H. Spurgeon on the subject.

binding Satan, and renouncing curses. While some don't give any thought to the activity of the unseen world, others are so consumed with it that they live in constant threat, fear, or even terror of their unseen enemy. The perspectives one can be exposed to in the realm of spiritual warfare practices range from the orthodox to the absurd.

Why another book on spiritual warfare? I believe the Bible describes true spiritual warfare. I believe many Christians lack a full and functioning understanding of what spiritual warfare truly is and how it is to be waged. With so much nonsense being taught across the Christian landscape, it is no wonder that God's people are confused. Too much teaching on this subject has no basis in Scripture and has more in common with pagan mysticism than anything biblical or Christian. I hope and pray that the time and energy invested in this book may be used by God to call His Church to Scripture as the guide for waging an effective spiritual battle.

We must go to the Bible and ask, "What am I told to do in order to be an effective soldier in this spiritual battle?" When we ask that question and allow the Bible to speak for itself, we avoid the pagan mysticism, the faithless superstition, and the terrifying preoccupation with the demonic. We avoid the unbiblical practices that have somehow wedded themselves to the church.

I believe this book will stretch your thinking, challenge some traditions, and for some of us, plow new ground for us as we seek to build a biblical theology of spiritual warfare. We will see that tradition, superstition, mysticism, our own thinking, or worse yet, the testimony of demons themselves, prove to be very poor foundations for theology.

A Personal Journey

Spiritual warfare is one subject that I have spent a lot of time wrestling through. I have undergone a reformation of sorts in which I had to jettison much of what I was taught and had absorbed as a new believer.

I understand that personal testimonies are, well, just that - personal. They are not objective. They are nothing more than anecdotal. We shouldn't build our theology on personal testimonies,

3

whether our own or someone else's. We must build our understanding of spiritual warfare on the Bible and the Bible alone. My own story helps to illustrate the need to reject all unbiblical and man-made practices.

At the time God saved me, I knew nothing about the Bible - nothing. I had memorized some passages of Scripture, but my knowledge of the background and teaching of Bible books was negligible. Though I attended church somewhat regularly before going off to Bible College, I still was not well-taught or discipled.

Bible College exposed me to a wide variety of diverse teachings and practices. It was not what I was taught in the classroom that shaped my theology of spiritual warfare, but what I picked up in my conversations and time with other students. The student body consisted of students from all kinds of backgrounds. Some were very charismatic and had been exposed to "power encounters" and "exorcisms."

With or without the approval of staff and teachers, certain books and tapes made the rounds through the student body as teachable, zealous, and ambitious young adults gobbled up nearly everything that had a Christian flavor to it without stopping to examine it against Scripture. We had zeal in abundance, passion in excess, but discernment in scarcity.

I heard students promoting practices such as praying a hedge of thorns, naming demons, renouncing past generational curses, and binding and rebuking Satan. There were even some people who promoted exorcisms as a legitimate means of warfare against Satan and his hosts. For the first time in my Christian life, I met folks who believed that Christians could be demon possessed.

Neil T. Anderson's books and teachings became common fare on the bookshelves and in the dorms. Many of his practices were adopted and promoted among the student body. Two books of Christian fiction were setting the Christian world on fire: *This Present Darkness* and *Piercing the Darkness*, by Frank Peretti. For some in the student body, these two books functioned as a manual for effective spiritual warfare. Books by converted occultists were passed around enthusiastically. After all, who could possibly think they were

equipped to do battle with demons if they had never read anything
by supposed "former satanists" like Mike Warnke and Rebecca
Brown?

I was also exposed to an audio tape which offered a
methodology for spiritual warfare promising the salvation of loved
ones for whom certain prayers were prayed. Who wouldn't want that?
The tape laid out a methodology which included binding Satan,
renouncing generational sins and curses, naming demons and
binding them, praying a hedge of thorns, and pleading the blood of
Jesus over people, places, and things.

It all sounded good to me - for a while. I prayed the prayers, I
pled the blood, I dutifully bound demons and rebuked Satan,
thinking that I was well on my way to spiritual victory and true
sanctification. I was waging real warfare! Or so I thought.

At the same time, I was learning in my classes about the
sovereignty of God, the limitations that Satan has, and what the Bible
teaches about sanctification in the Christian life. For a long while I
was able to compartmentalize my theology, not seeing that what I
learned in the classroom did not mesh well with what I practiced in
the dorm.

Now don't get me wrong, I was not some wacky charismatic
demon hunter trying to cast demons out of every object. I didn't
perform exorcisms or see visions of demons or anything like that, but
I had imbibed a theology of the demonic that did not mesh with
Scripture. The day came when I finally realized that what I was
learning from Scripture in my classes did not match what I was
learning from other books and students in my dorm.

My change in thinking started when I overheard some
discussions among the Fourth Year students about what they were
learning in their class on Christian living, which that particular week,
covered the subject of spiritual warfare. They spoke of the amazing
things they were learning - things they had never thought of before.
Suddenly, the pieces were coming together for them and they were
realizing that what they had believed for so long was wrong. It now
seemed so ridiculous and out of step with Scripture. They spoke of
being liberated from so much superstition and fear.

I heard one student, whom I loved and respected, mention that "binding Satan" was a completely unbiblical practice.

"What makes you say that?" I asked.

He began to share with me what he was learning in his class on spiritual warfare. I realized that what he was sharing with me was a perspective and worldview which I had learned in class, but never translated to practice. I listened and offered a few arguments and questions. I wasn't trying to refute him, but I did want some more information. What he was sharing seemed so simple, practical, and, above all, biblical. Nothing he said contradicted what I had learned in my classes. The light started to dawn and I began to see some contradictions in my own thinking.

I started to ask questions of some of the other Fourth Year students. Finally one of them said, "You just need to read the book."

"What book?! How do I get my hands on this book?"

On his recommendation, I made my way to the campus book store and bought *A Holy Rebellion,* by Thomas Ice and Robert Dean Jr.[4] I devoured that book. I read and re-read nearly every chapter in a short period of time. I compared it to Scripture and found that, unlike my previous theology of spiritual warfare, this book offered a perspective that fit with what I was learning from the Bible. I couldn't argue with it. I found myself saying, "Yeah, that's right. That makes so much sense. How come I didn't think of that? How could I not see that?"

Over the course of a couple of short months, I went through a radical reformation in my thinking. I came to understand that the Bible and the Bible alone serves as our guide in the area of spiritual warfare. I was liberated from a mystic, superstitious approach to spiritual warfare as suddenly as if a light had been turned on. I started to see as folly what I had thought was biblical. It all began to make sense.

---

[4] I probably read that book five times before I was ever required to read it in Fourth Year. It contained all my notes, observations, highlighting and scribbles from all my study, research and meditation. It was so worn it was nearly falling apart! I lent it to someone and I can't remember whom. Subsequently, the book was republished under the title *Overrun By Demons: The Church's Preoccupation with the Demonic.* Now it is currently published under the title *What the Bible Teaches About Spiritual Warfare* by Kregel Publications.

How Will You Respond?

I know that among those who read this book there will be some who were liberated long ago from their preoccupation with the demonic. Like me, you once thought that real spiritual warfare consisted of doing hand-to-hand combat with demons to take back territory Satan had conquered. At one time your view of spiritual warfare had more in common with Frank Peretti's *This Present Darkness* than with anything I present in this book. You left all that behind. Due to the teaching of Scripture, through some means, you came to understand that real spiritual warfare is not about TERRITORY but TRUTH. I trust that you will find this book encouraging, affirming, and equipping.

Others who read this book are still where I once was. You have been taught that spiritual warfare is about taking back territory from Satan. You have been instructed to pray a hedge of thorns, name demons, and bind Satan. You have never thought through some of these things and never been challenged in your thinking. The fact that these things aren't taught in Scripture is going to be completely new to you. You have never questioned the assumptions or the practices that result from them. Much of what I have to say will shock you.

Do one thing for me: test it all by Scripture (Acts 17:11). Go to the Scriptures and see if what I say from the text of the Bible is true or not. Rightly interpret. Give due diligence. Think it through. Examine and test everything I say and everything you believe. The truth will win.

Still others will read this book who have never heard of binding Satan, pleading the blood, praying a hedge, territorial spirits, naming demons, or generational curses. This is all new to you. In that case, do one thing for me: test it all by Scripture (Acts 17:11). If you haven't heard of these things before, you will. You need to give some careful consideration to what the Bible teaches on these matters so you are not caught off guard or deceived.

Some will be encouraged. Some will feel a sense of liberation as old perspectives give way to a new approach to spiritual warfare - one they had never considered. Some, hopefully a small number, will be angry, feeling that their favorite teachers have been attacked and their discernment questioned. Some will feel as if I am trying to rob them of their most precious tools in the fight against evil. I am not. Actually, I am trying to equip you with tools - biblical tools - so that together we may "resist in the evil day" (Ephesians 6:13).

Part 1:
Establishing Biblical
Principles

1

Our Source of Intelligence

It is a well known maxim of warfare that you must "know thy enemy." Ancient Chinese military general Sun Tzu said, "If you know the enemy and know yourself, you need not fear the results of a hundred battles." He also said, "Know thy self, know thy enemy. A thousand battles, a thousand victories."[1]

War cannot be waged without intelligence. Commanders in the field have to know the location, direction, and intention of their enemy. Nations spend billions of dollars each year gathering intelligence on known and potential enemies. The nation with superior intelligence has a greater chance of winning the war. Handicap a nation's ability to gather intelligence and you handicap its ability to fight an effective war.

We are engaged in a war. It is not a war against flesh and blood, but against principalities, powers, against spiritual forces in heavenly places (Ephesians 6:10-12). The stakes are high, the battles are real, and the enemy is a mighty one. In fact, he is stronger, smarter, and more adept at winning this war than we are. We need intelligence about our enemy to effectively engage the battle. After all, we don't want to be fighting the wrong battle in the wrong way with the wrong means! That would mean certain defeat.

A nation engaged in a war can gather intelligence from a number of sources. They might rely upon satellite photos, surveillance planes, spies, inside operatives, or traitors from the other side. They may glean valuable information from leaks, intercepted communications, anonymous tips, wire taps, or captured enemy combatants. These and a host of other means are all fair game in the world of modern warfare.

---

[1] Sun Tzu is believed to be the author of *The Art of War*.

Where do we get our intelligence for the battle that we wage? The Bible.

The Bible Alone!

That's it. One source. No others.

We have only one source of intelligence that we are commanded to use. All our information comes from one channel. We have nowhere else to turn, no other source.

If you are responding with incredulity right now, your view of Scripture is far too low. If you are among the many who would be tempted to think, "Man. That's it? I am doomed. If that is all I have, then I might as well give up now," your view of the Bible and its sufficiency is deficient.

Your response should be, "No problem, because that is all I need."

What else could you need? The God who wrote the Bible cannot lie (Titus 1:2) so we can be assured that all the information that He has given is absolutely true. Further, He knows infinitely more about angels, demons, and the spiritual battle than any other source could ever hope to offer. He knows the path to victory. He knows the past, present, and future perfectly. He knows the outcome and has assured that outcome. He knows the enemy better than the enemy knows himself. God also knows each one of us: our weaknesses, our needs, and our frailties. We have the one absolutely perfect, reliable, and trustworthy source for all intelligence.

I doubt that many would question my assertions regarding God and His Word. The danger is not that you and I would *deny* these truths in the area of spiritual warfare, but that we might fail to *apply* these truths in the area of spiritual warfare. No true believer would ever question God's omniscience or His truthfulness. However, believers do fail to understand how these truths should inform our view of spiritual warfare.

Is the Bible Enough?

All errors in Christian theology and practice can be traced back to an inadequate view of Scripture. The modern church's low view of Scripture is evidenced by its willingness to dabble with psychology, its readiness to absent the Bible from the preaching ministry, and its constant pursuit and embrace of extra biblical revelation.[2]

The doctrine of the sufficiency of Scripture is so foundational to Christian theology and practice that we find ourselves drawn back to it time and again. Before we can build a theology of spiritual warfare, we must first establish a firm understanding of and commitment to the sufficiency of Scripture. We will see in the chapters to follow, errant belief and practice in the realm of spiritual warfare has its genesis in a failure to derive theology from Scripture alone. Sadly, there is no sphere of the Christian life where this doctrine gets jettisoned more quickly than it does in the theology behind modern spiritual warfare practices.

In the chapters that follow, we will have to come back to a basic theology of Scripture and ask, "How does this apply to spiritual warfare?" All errant theology regarding spiritual warfare methodology is a result of failing to apply the doctrine of the sufficiency of Scripture to this subject. All the silly practices, all the preoccupation with demons, and all the pagan mysticism masquerading as truth, result from the practical denial of the sufficiency of Scripture.

We begin where we must, with the Bible. We have to be reminded of what the Bible says concerning itself.

The Sufficient Source of Truth

When we affirm the Bible to be the only reliable source of information regarding angels, demons, and spiritual warfare, we are not asserting something of the Bible that the Bible does not claim for itself. How do we know the Bible is sufficient and reliable? Let's take a look at just a couple of key passages.

2 Timothy 3:16-17: "All Scripture is inspired by God and profitable for teaching, for reproof, for correction, for training in

---

[2] I am writing a book on this subject titled *God Doesn't Whisper* which will be available in 2019.

righteousness; so that the man of God may be adequate, equipped for every good work."[3]

The Apostle Paul described the Scriptures as "inspired" and "profitable." Paul told young Timothy, Scripture is "inspired" or literally "God-breathed" (θεόπνευστος). The NASB translates it as "inspired," but the NIV better translates it as "God-breathed." That is to say the product you hold in your hand was given by the breath of God Himself. This is the claim the Bible makes for itself.

When we affirm that the Scriptures are God-breathed, we do not mean that the Bible *contains* the Word of God (as if God's Word is found somewhere within Scripture).[4] We do not mean that the Bible *becomes* the Word of God when we read it or experience it personally.[5] Rather, *it is* the Word of God - whether men believe it, obey it, and trust it or not. It is an objective, revealed truth from the God of the universe Who has not only given us His Word but preserved and protected His Word. Consequently, we have the very words of God's revelation.

Since the Bible is God-breathed, it is the inerrant, infallible, true, and accurate source of information regarding life, eternity, history, reality, God, salvation, Heaven, Hell, and the unseen world of angels and demons. God cannot lie (Titus 1:2).

Therefore, the Scriptures are to be believed, trusted and obeyed. Scripture is not a collection of archaic observations by religious men collected over hundreds of years. The Bible is God's Word - holy, infallible, and true. Of the many sources available to us by which we might get information concerning the spiritual realm, the Bible alone is vouchsafed as absolutely inerrant.

---

[3] All Scripture quotations in this work are taken from the New American Standard Bible (NASB) 1995 Update (La Habra, Lockman Foundation, 1995) unless otherwise noted.

[4] Some teach that within the pages of Scripture, hidden in the words, or hidden in the teachings of the Bible, the Word of God is mystically contained. They would say that it is then up to us to read and experience the Scriptures in order that we might discover the Word of God contained within them.

[5] This idea was popularized by the neo-orthodox movement of the mid twentieth century which taught that when the Bible is experienced and passages "come alive," then, and only then, do they *become* the Word of God to us. That is a hopelessly relativistic approach that Paul would have rejected.

The second word Paul used to describe Scripture is "profitable" (ὠφέλιμος). The word means "useful." The Scriptures are useful "for teaching, for reproof, for correction, for training in righteousness." When the Word of God is used in this way it results in the man (or woman) of God being "adequate, equipped for every good work." The word "equipped" (from ἐξαρτίζω) means "to make someone completely adequate or sufficient for something; to furnish completely; to cause to be fully qualified; adequacy."[6] The Word of God equips the Christian, making him adequate for life, ministry, and certainly the spiritual battle.

What do you need to make you adequate for spiritual warfare? What provides you with all the tools necessary to fight the battle? All we need is the God-breathed Scriptures which equip and mature the man of God for all areas of life and service. If we have Scripture, we have all that is necessary, and need nothing more. We have to get that truth ingrained deep in our souls. Countless teachings on spiritual warfare direct us to look elsewhere for information about the enemy and the tactics to fight him.

In earthly warfare between nations, intelligence has to be constantly vetted, analyzed, and verified before it is trusted. Those who gather intelligence have to constantly ask if a photograph has been faked, if the tip is legitimate and if the source is trustworthy. We need not doubt for one moment our source of intelligence because it is the very Word of the God of Truth.

Like Paul, Peter pointed his readers to the Scriptures as the sufficient, God-given revelation of truth. 2 Peter 1:3-4: ". . . seeing that His divine power has granted to us everything pertaining to life and godliness, through the true knowledge of Him who called us by His own glory and excellence. For by these He has granted to us His precious and magnificent promises, so that by them you may become partakers of the divine nature, having escaped the corruption that is in the world by lust."

---

6 J.P. & Nida Louw, E. A., *Vol. 1: Greek-English lexicon of the New Testament: Based on semantic domains* (electronic ed. of the 2nd edition) (New York: United Bible Societies, 1996), 679.

God has granted[7] us everything pertaining to life and godliness. All we need we have been given in Christ. We came to a true knowledge of Him who called us and we were saved, becoming partakers of the divine nature and escaping the corruption that is in the world by lust.

By His glory and excellence, God granted us everything necessary for life and godliness. That is a statement on the complete sufficiency of Scripture in the life of a Christian. We have been granted salvation by His calling. We have been given all that is necessary to live the Christian life. This complete sufficiency is found in His precious and magnificent promises - His Word. All God has promised us we find in His Word.

Between our salvation in Christ and the Word of Christ we have our complete sufficiency. What else could we possibly need? When we consider the rich blessing of God's Word, the salvation we have been granted, and the fact that we are partakers in the nature of God through the indwelling Holy Spirit, can we really say, "Ah, that's nice, but it's not enough. I need more."? No! That is an insult to divine grace and to the Word of God.

It Is All We NEED

In affirming the Bible is sufficient as the source of intelligence in our spiritual battle, we are not saying the Bible contains all that CAN be known. God has not revealed everything there is to know about Himself, His will, Heaven, Hell, angels and demons. However, He has revealed all we NEED to know and all He wants us to know.

God has not told us everything that is going on in these realms [spiritual realms], but He has told us all that we need to know to protect ourselves and carry out our mission successfully. When we begin to rely on information based on sources other than the Bible, we may

---

[7] This is a perfect tense indicating something that is past and completed. It is not something that continues or needs to be repeated. It cannot be duplicated, added to, or improved upon.

render ourselves vulnerable because we have unknowingly overstepped our bounds.[8]

The Bible does not claim to be the only source of all truth[9], or to reveal all that can be known about these subjects.[10] The Bible does claim to give us true and accurate information and it does claim to give us all the information we need for any and every situation that arises in our lives.[11]

Now for the Rub

I doubt many, if any, of the people who read this book would reject the inerrancy and infallibility of Scripture. I assume that most readers would readily affirm all that I have said concerning Scripture thus far. You likely have a high view of Scripture.

The danger we face in the realm of spiritual warfare is not that we would *deny* the authority and reliability of Scripture outright, but that we would fail to *apply* that belief. As Ice and Dean write,

. . . even among those who affirm the inerrancy and infallibility of Scripture, many Christians deny this authority of Scripture in the way they apply (or fail to apply) Scripture to their daily lives. Many Christians do not seem to view the Bible as sufficient for every good work when we look at certain practices which they have built upon viewpoints found outside the Bible. This is especially true in the area of spiritual warfare.[12]

We must constantly return to Scripture to build our thinking and practice on the Bible alone. We need to challenge commonly held

---

[8] Thomas Ice and Robert Dean, Jr., *Overrun By Demons: The Church's New Preoccupation With the Demonic* (Eugene: Harvest House Publishers, 1990), 20.

[9] For instance, the Bible does not claim to be a complete source for all truth about oceanography, architecture, quantum physics, or mathematics. But where the Bible speaks, it always speaks truth and cannot err.

[10] We are not told what demons look like, what they are named, if they are named, or how they are structured. There is a lot about angels and demons that we are not told in Scripture and that is by God's design and wisdom.

[11] Ice and Dean, 22.

[12] Ibid., 22-23.

practices and beliefs with Scripture and test all things against the Word of God. We should seek to build our theology of demons, demon possession, demon exorcism, and spiritual warfare on Scripture and Scripture alone.

Bad Methodology

There are two approaches commonly employed by Christians in building their theology of spiritual warfare.

The first method we can call "*the empirical method*." This method is the most prevalent in our day. The empirical approach seeks to learn as much as possible about demons, demonic possession, and how to fight demons from any source. People who have been demonized or spent time in the occult are interviewed. Information is gathered. Experiences are collated and mined for details. It is not uncommon to find people building entire theologies and practices based on information gleaned from ex-Satanists, witches, or even from an interview with a demon itself! The empirical method gathers data from observations and experiences.

The second method is to base our understanding on revelation. We study the Bible and the Bible alone! Is that too simple for you? Does this method strike you as inadequate, antiquated, and passe?

I favor this method!

When the first method is employed and we base our theology on experiences, there is no end to the silly theology and unbiblical practices that inevitably result.

For instance, I have heard people claim that when dealing with demons you need to give them specific commands. Not any old command will do, but you have to command them "in the name of Jesus the Christ, the Son of God." They claim there are demons named "Jesus," so it does no good to command demons in the name of Jesus because if you don't specify which Jesus, then you are just calling upon the name of one of the demons named Jesus.

Does the Bible say there are demons named Jesus? No. So how do these folks know there are demons named Jesus? People who are "authorities" in the realm of spiritual warfare will tell you they have exorcised demons named Jesus. They have talked with demons named Jesus. This is information gleaned from demons! Is it reliable information? Hardly. It is a theology and practice based on an experience coupled with information gleaned from a demon.

Someone will counter, "But the person performing the exorcism commanded the demon to tell the truth 'in the name of Jesus Christ the Son of God and by the power of His blood.' If you command them to tell the truth by the name and blood of Jesus, they have to tell the truth."

Does Scripture say this? No. Again, how would they know? They were told by a demon this is how you get demons to tell the truth. Once again, they are basing their practice on experience and demonic testimony.

None of these concepts are even remotely based on Scripture. It is quite laughable, and yet, Christians buy it hook, line, and sinker. You can find books on the subject of spiritual warfare by the hundreds. These authors will affirm on one page the authority and sufficiency of Scripture and on the next page promote a methodology of spiritual warfare based not on a single verse of Scripture, but on their experience, their interviews, and their encounters with demons.

Techniques and information gleaned from demons being taught as though it were the truth of God is the highest form of blasphemy. It dishonors God, besmirches His Word, and impugns His character. These are doctrines of demons (1 Timothy 4:1) being taught as if they are the truth of God. To treat the testimony of demons as if it were as pure, trustworthy, and true as the Word of God itself is blasphemy, pure and simple.

> Anytime we base a technique for dealing with demonized people on anything other than the clear teaching of the Word of God, we are doomed to failure. In fact, using any approach based on information not directly derived from the Scriptures is in practice a denial of the authority and sufficiency of Scripture.[13]

It is absolutely crucial that in the area of spiritual warfare we build our theology on the Bible and the Bible alone. Let me be as clear,

---

[13] Ibid., 34.

concise, straightforward, and gracious as I possibly can. I don't care what you have experienced. I don't care what someone you know has experienced. I don't care what your cousin's mother's best friend's uncle's missionary brother has experienced in some remote tribe somewhere in the distant reaches of the Amazon jungle. I don't care what some popular spiritual warfare "expert" says, or what experience suggests, or what a demon has said, or what an ex-Satanist knows. Neither should you!

We have a perfect source of truth that provides all that we need to fight the battle. Everything must be based on Scripture and Scripture alone. In the pages to come you will see just how far some have strayed from this first principle. May God keep us in His Word!

2

Truth or Territory?

Having established that Scripture is our only reliable source of information about the spiritual realm, we now need to define "spiritual warfare." Spiritual warfare is the most widely misunderstood subject in modern evangelicalism. When most Christians hear or read the words "spiritual warfare," they envision some sort of mystical hand-to-hand combat that is waged with demons by certain types of prayers, mantras, incantations, or practices such as binding Satan, praying a hedge of thorns, exorcisms, or rebuking demons in an attempt to take territory from Satan and claim it for Christ.

Not only are these specific practices not the least bit biblical,[1] but neither is the notion that spiritual warfare involves direct interaction against demons in order to gain spiritual or physical territory.

We can only look to Scripture for a description of spiritual warfare and allow the Bible to define this warfare for us. We must not adopt occultic, mystical practices or worldviews. We are not free to make up practices that we think would be effective in the spiritual battle. We can only turn to the Bible and allow God to tell us what constitutes real spiritual warfare. Consequently, any practice not founded upon a sound interpretation of biblical texts in their context must be rejected. All our thinking and understanding of spiritual warfare must be grounded in Scripture.

---

[1] We will examine these practices and the passages that are used to support them in the following chapters.

A Biblical Description of Spiritual Warfare

We turn to a familiar passage - one that is often quoted but seldom rightly understood.

> For though we walk in the flesh, we do not war according to the flesh, for the weapons of our warfare are not of the flesh, but divinely powerful for the destruction of fortresses. We are destroying speculations and every lofty thing raised up against the knowledge of God, and we are taking every thought captive to the obedience of Christ, and we are ready to punish all disobedience, whenever your obedience is complete (2 Corinthians 10:3-5).

Perhaps you were expecting Ephesians 6 and a discussion on the armor of God, or some passage from the gospels where Jesus commanded and exorcised demons. We will deal with those passages in time, but we begin at a more foundational level and answer the question: "What is spiritual warfare?"

In 2 Corinthians 10, the Apostle Paul defines and describes the essence of spiritual warfare. In these verses, he tells us how we fight, what we fight, and why we fight. In 2 Corinthians 10, we have a definition and description of spiritual warfare which plays a critical role in equipping us to engage our enemy.

As with any Bible text, we need to give some attention to the context in order to ensure we are rightly understanding the meaning of the passage.

Paul wrote 2 Corinthians as a defense of himself, his co-workers and his ministry. After writing 1 Corinthians, some people in the church at Corinth had started what can only be described as a character assassination campaign against Paul. There were men in Corinth who claimed to be apostles. They were apparently very talented, gifted, and persuasive men whose constant attacks on Paul swayed the hearts and loyalties of the Corinthian believers. These false teachers impugned Paul's motives. They claimed he was in ministry for the money. They said Paul lacked integrity. They suggested he was a hypocrite who said one thing and did another. Even the people who worked and served with Paul were not immune from their attacks. These charlatans attacked Titus and impugned his motives. They claimed that neither Paul nor Titus had God-given authority. They mocked Paul's physical appearance, his abilities, and his preaching.

Paul responded with a blistering description of these men as "false apostles, deceitful workers, disguising themselves as apostles of Christ" (2 Corinthians 11:13-15). He said that since Satan appears as an angel of light, so too his (Satan's) servants would likewise appear as servants of Christ. Rather than being messengers of Christ, they were, in reality, demonically inspired and empowered false teachers - messengers from Satan.[2]

Paul wrote 2 Corinthians to defend himself and his co-workers against the attacks of the false teachers. He defended Titus, who traveled with him, reminding the Corinthians of Titus's integrity, willingness to work, and blameless life. He defended his own apostleship, authority, power, ministry, conduct, motives, and, most importantly, the message of the gospel - which Paul contended was the truth. Occasionally Paul quoted his Corinthian critics. For instance,

> For even if I boast somewhat further about our authority, which the Lord gave for building you up and not for destroying you, I will not be put to shame, for I do not wish to seem as if I would terrify you by my letters. For they say, "His letters are weighty and strong, but his personal presence is unimpressive and his speech contemptible" (2 Corinthians 10:8-10).

His critics were saying, "Paul sure can write a strong letter for being such a weak and unimpressive person. He's not so tough. He is not even that great of an orator. He is contemptible and his speech is pathetic."

Paul was planning a trip to Corinth to deal with these issues in person, though he certainly didn't want to. In fact, he hoped that the Corinthians would deal with this nightmare before he arrived.

---

[2] I believe that these false teachers, and one in particular, was Paul's "thorn in the flesh." These were messengers of Satan who proved a constant source of pain for Paul.

In the beginning of this chapter Paul said,

Now I, Paul, myself urge you by the meekness and gentleness of Christ - I who am meek when face to face with you, but bold toward you when absent! I ask that when I am present I need not be bold with the confidence with which I propose to be courageous against some, who regard us as if we walked according to the flesh (2 Corinthians 10:1-2).

If they said Paul was strong in his letters, wait till the little man showed up in Corinth! He told them in verse 2, he hoped he would not need to be as bold and strong in confronting them as he was intending to be. This was a warning! "You deal with this situation before I arrive or I will deal with it, and if I deal with it, you are not going to like it!"

In verse 6 of Chapter 10, Paul said he was "ready to punish all disobedience, whenever your obedience is complete." The obedience Paul had in mind in this Corinthian situation was a wholesale rejection of these men, their methods, and their attacks on Paul. If the church was willing to reject these men and reaffirm Paul and his message and ministry, then Paul would come and punish the disobedience of these men.

In verse 2, Paul said he was coming and it was not going to be pretty. In verse 6, Paul said that he was coming to punish all disobedience. Sandwiched in between those verses is this text on spiritual warfare. In verses 3-5 Paul drew a stark comparison between *his* method of ministry and that of these *"other men."* Paul described his own ministry, contrasting it with the ministry of these false teachers.

With all that context and background, let's look at these verses in detail and see *how* we fight, *what* we fight, and *why* we fight.

The "How" of Our Warfare

The false teachers in Corinth claimed Paul's methodology and tactics in ministry were fleshly and worldly. They labeled Paul's ministry as "not spiritual enough." They said it was "fleshly" and wasn't dealing with real spiritual issues. According to them, Paul wasn't doing real spiritual battle, but only engaging on a fleshly level.

He answered in verse 3-4, "For though we walk in the flesh, we do not war according to the flesh, for the weapons of our warfare are not of the flesh, but divinely powerful for the destruction of fortresses."

The word "flesh" here is not used in its ethical or moral sense. Paul is not saying we walk "carnally" or "immorally." It is used in its normal, more literal sense, meaning "we are normal men." He simply meant that he participated in normal human existence with all of its inherent limitations. Fortunately, our method of doing battle is not limited by our physical nature or our human frailties. We do not wage war merely according to the flesh.[3] Though we walk physically, we battle spiritually.

God has given us certain weapons which are to be used in spiritual warfare. Since the battle we fight is not a physical battle, but a spiritual one, the weapons we employ are likewise spiritual and not physical. When Paul says that the "weapons of our warfare are not of the flesh," he means that they are not of human making or design. We have heavenly weapons, given by God for the advance of truth, not designed by men for the defense of territory.

Paul highlighted a very real temptation that we often face, namely to approach our life, walk, ministry, or warfare from a purely human vantage point. We walk in this world and we are constantly bombarded with the best of human wisdom, human methodologies, human thinking and worldly ways. We are surrounded by new and improved theories of how ministry is to be done, how demons are to be fought, how the Christian life is to be lived. We are often told that we can accomplish divine ends with worldly means. Nothing could be further from the truth!

---

[3] This passage is loaded with military imagery. The warfare imagery was a favorite for Paul. Ephesians 6 contains a lot of warfare imagery and the battle armor of a Roman Soldier is used as an object lesson for Christian battle. We see similar imagery in 2 Timothy 2:3-4, "Suffer hardship with me, as a good soldier of Christ Jesus. No soldier in active service entangles himself in the affairs of everyday life, so that he may please the one who enlisted him as a soldier." See also 2 Timothy 4:7 and Jude 3 for references to fighting. Paul viewed the Christian life as a long battle, a long struggle, a constant fight.

In coming chapters we will address methods of spiritual warfare which are completely of men's making and not God-given at all. Spiritual warfare "how-to manuals" are filled with tactics and methods which are birthed in the minds and thinking of men and demons and not derived from the Word of God. We have to make sure our "weapons" are not of human origin.

Though we walk here in the flesh, we do not use fleshly means to accomplish God's end. A read through 1 and 2 Corinthians gives us some examples of "fleshly weapons." The Corinthians trusted in human wisdom and human understanding which they elevated above divine wisdom. They cherished displays of human abilities, gifts, and talents. They criticized Paul because he was not as gifted in oratory as others. They formed divisions around different teachers and boasted in their own abilities. They sought approval from men and large followings. These are the types of fleshly weapons Paul rejected. In fact, in 1 Corinthians 1, Paul revealed that when he came to Corinth, he purposely refused to engage the Corinthians on that level, even though he knew that he could gain a following if he adopted such man-centered methods of ministry. Instead, he opted for the foolishness of preaching and the wisdom of God, the very opposite of what was sure to draw a following in Corinth.[4]

Satan loves to deceive us into using methods that are fleshly - gimmicks, campaigns, and publicity stunts (methods of our own making) - and to abandon the weapons that God gives us which are divinely powerful.

Did you notice in this passage that Paul does not tell us what our weapons are? He does give us some clues. So far we have seen three things about our weapons.

First, they are spiritual not fleshly.

Second, the weapons are mighty in God. They pack divine power. That cannot be said for any human methodology or wisdom; they never carry divine power.

Third, these weapons destroy strongholds. They destroy fortresses. They are "divinely powerful for the destruction of

---

[4] 1 Corinthians 1:18-2:9.

fortresses" (v. 4). That brings us to the next issue: against what are our weapons aimed?

The "What" of Our Warfare

You might still be wondering what these weapons are. What spiritual weapon do we have which is given by God, endued with His power, and can destroy fortresses? Before we can answer that question, we have to find out what these fortresses are. What is it we are fighting? What is the target? Are we fighting the ACLU, the homosexual lobby, abortion doctors, or political parties? Who is our enemy? What are our weapons aimed at?

2 Corinthians 10:4 gives us the answer: "For the weapons of our warfare are not of the flesh, but divinely powerful *for the destruction of fortresses.*" What are these fortresses we are to destroy in spiritual warfare?

Some say these fortresses are demonic strongholds, heavenly power structures, generational curses, incantations, demonic hierarchies. They therefore conclude that our weapons involve methods and means which are intended to weaken demonic power, hinder the devil, release people from curses, pray down these strongholds, and ward off spirits.

How does Paul describe these fortresses? He says that "we are destroying speculations and every lofty thing raised up against the knowledge of God, and we are taking every thought captive to the obedience of Christ" (10:5). He uses the words "speculations," "knowledge of God," and "thought." Those words tell us all we need to know about the nature of spiritual warfare.

The word translated "speculations" or "arguments" (NASB, NIV) means "thoughts" or "imaginations." It refers to "reasonings" or "thought processes." The fortresses we are destroying are not physical fortresses. They are not demonic mantras, spells, or curses. They are not demonic hierarchical power structures. The fortresses are *mental* fortresses. We destroy "thoughts" and "reasonings."

The next phrase further describes these fortresses as "every lofty thing raised up against the knowledge of God." "Lofty thing" shows the pride of these mental fortresses. The term "lofty thing" was used

27

to describe the towers that would encompass military fortresses. The towers would rise high into the sky and provide defense.

These mental fortresses are against the knowledge of God. Paul is not just describing innocent thoughts. He is talking about mental fortresses, reasonings of the human heart, prideful, self-reliant, man-centered human philosophies and speculations. The war we wage is against the proud, lofty, God-defying speculations of the human heart that are raised up in opposition to the true knowledge of God.

Man's Mental Fortresses

Mankind is surrounded by the knowledge of God. He has knowledge of God in creation and he chooses to suppress that truth in unrighteousness.[5] While not hearing any audible voice, man is surrounded by God's creation which ceaselessly testifies to its Creator.[6] Men have knowledge of God revealed in their conscience which constantly accuses them of breaking the law of God written on their hearts.[7] How does man respond to the light of creation and conscience? He suppresses the truth in unrighteousness because he loves darkness rather than light.[8] Man's intellect is darkened and his mind is at enmity against God.[9] Instead of submitting to the truth, men erect mental fortresses which keep them hostage and safe in unbelief. They hole up in their lofty, pride-filled thinking which insulates them against the knowledge of God. These fortresses consist of worldly arguments, reasonings, science (falsely so called), thoughts, and philosophies which militantly stand, raised up, hostile to God and the true knowledge of Him.

Wishing to be the center of his own self-sufficient universe, man in his unregenerate state does not want to turn from his sin or submit his pride-filled heart to the Sovereign God. He holds himself hostage in his mental fortress surrounded by his reasons for unbelief. His

---

[5] Romans 1:21ff.

[6] Psalm 19:1-6.

[7] Romans 2:12-16.

[8] John 3:19-21; Romans 1:18ff.

[9] Romans 8:6-8.

towers of "philosophy," "knowledge," "science," and "evolution" form his defense against the truth.

To the unregenerate man, insulated from the knowledge of God by his mental fortress, the preaching of the cross is foolishness.[10] Men, in partnership with the forces of darkness, erect all kinds of "speculations" and "lofty thoughts" against the truth. Evolution, atheism, moral relativism, tolerance, political correctness, theological liberalism, rationalism, naturalism, humanism and many others are examples of Satanic deceptions erected in the minds and hearts of men.

Man willingly believes anything but the truth and he uses the lies offered by Satan to build the bulwarks against it. Satan is pleased because he works to entrench men in error while blinding them to the truth. Man loves the darkness and hates the light and so he gladly settles in behind his lofty imaginations and speculations.

Philip Hughes describes Christian warfare this way:

Hence it is that the Christian warfare is aimed at the casting down of the reasonings which are the strongholds whereby the unbelieving mind seeks to fortify itself against the truths of human depravity and divine grace, and at the casting down also of every proud bulwark raised high against the knowledge of God.[11]

A war is waging for the truth. Satan, the great liar and murderer from the beginning, deceives men with his crafty lies. He and his host of demon helpers are constantly promoting, teaching, and advancing their lies. These lies are the proud speculations of the human mind and heart.

We are at war over truth! Spiritual warfare is a truth war. We fight lies by advancing truth. When truth advances, God is glorified and the forces of darkness suffer defeat.

---

[10] 1 Corinthians 1:18ff.

[11] Philip Edgcumbe Hughes, *The New International Commentary on the New Testament, The Second Epistle to the Corinthians* (Grand Rapids: Wm. B. Eerdmans Publishing Co., 1962), 352.

How do we fight? We fight a spiritual war with spiritual weapons. What are we fighting? We are fighting the reasonings, thoughts, and speculations of error erected in the hearts of men.

Now some related questions: What are our weapons? What is "mighty in God for the destruction of fortresses?" What does God use to destroy error and advance truth? What contains divine truth able to pierce right to the heart, bring conviction, remove blindness, destroy human wisdom, confound the wise, and bring people to a knowledge of the truth? The Word of God.

The gospel and the Word of God are the means of waging true spiritual warfare. Once we understand that true spiritual warfare is a war over the truth, then we are left with little doubt as to the identity of our weapon. It is the gospel of truth contained in the Word of Truth.

With this understanding as a background, read the following familiar verses.

For I am not ashamed of the gospel, for it is the power of God for salvation to everyone who believes. . . (Romans 1:16).

For the word of the cross is foolishness to those who are perishing, but to us who are being saved it is the power of God. For it is written, "I WILL DESTROY THE WISDOM OF THE WISE, AND THE CLEVERNESS OF THE CLEVER I WILL SET ASIDE." Where is the wise man? Where is the scribe? Where is the debater of this age? Has not God made foolish the wisdom of the world? For since the wisdom of God the world through its wisdom did not come to know God, God was well-pleased through the foolishness of the message preached to save those who believe. For indeed Jews ask for signs and Greeks search for wisdom; but we preach Christ crucified, to the Jews a stumbling block and to Gentiles foolishness, but to those who are the called, both Jews and Greeks, Christ the power of God and the wisdom of God (1 Corinthians 1:18, 23-24).

Can you see the spiritual warfare language in these passages? God destroys human wisdom which is against the knowledge of God. He does this through the Word preached. The gospel is powerful for the destruction of these fortresses. It is powerful under God to bring every thought captive to Christ.

God does not use man's fleshly methods to wage this spiritual warfare. God uses the one tool that He has endued with divine power - His Word. The preaching of the Word and the preaching of the gospel is not a fleshly weapon of human origin. It does not rely upon the wisdom of man for its effectiveness! This weapon of truth is "not according to the flesh."

Paul described his preaching ministry in Corinth in 1 Corinthians 2:1-5.

> And when I came to you, brethren, I did not come with superiority of speech or of wisdom, proclaiming to you the testimony of God. [12] For I determined to know nothing among you except Jesus Christ, and Him crucified. I was with you in weakness and in fear and in much trembling, and my message and my preaching were not in persuasive words of wisdom, but in demonstration of the Spirit and of power, so that your faith would not rest on the wisdom of men, but on the power of God.

If Paul had wanted to use weapons of the flesh, he would have used "persuasive words of wisdom." He would have tried to impress the Corinthians with his oratory and rhetoric. Paul did not rely upon those fleshly means, however impressive they might have been to the Corinthians' worldly sensibilities. He preached the truth of the gospel in the power of the Spirit.

In 2 Corinthians 6:3 Paul defended his ministry so it "would not be discredited." He described the difficulties he had endured in ministry. Yet in the midst of afflictions, hardships, and distresses, Paul's ministry was "in purity, in knowledge, in patience, in kindness, in the Holy Spirit, in genuine love, in the word of truth, in the power

---

[12] Those would have been fleshly weapons.

of God; by the weapons of righteousness for the right hand and the left" (2 Corinthians 6:4-7).

One of the elements of the armor of God is the "sword of the spirit, which is the word of God."[13] Paul was a true and effective warrior in the spiritual realm. He was always concerned with the truth of the gospel and its faithful proclamation. In the context of discussing spiritual warfare, Paul requested prayer that "utterance may be given to me in the opening of my mouth, to make known with boldness the mystery of the gospel, for which I am an ambassador in chains; that in proclaiming it I may speak boldly, as I ought to speak" (Ephesians 6:18-20).

Gospel proclamation is powerful in God unto salvation. It delivers people from the kingdom of darkness to the kingdom of light, from error to truth, from Satan to God.

The "Why" of Our Warfare

Paul explains the reason we engage in the battle for truth in verse 5: ". . . we are taking every thought captive to the obedience of Christ" (2 Corinthians 10:5).

The word translated "thought" at the end of this passage is different from the word at the beginning of our passage translated "speculation." The word translated "thought" was used to describe the motive and intent of the mind. You could say we are fighting in order to bring every intention, every thought, and every device of the mind into obedience to Christ.

Who are we taking captive? We are taking as captives the very ones who once locked themselves in their mental fortresses. Once disobedient to Christ, held up in their castle of lies, the gospel is mighty in God to destroy their vain speculations and make them prisoners of Christ.

This Is Not What We Typically See!

This biblical description of spiritual warfare is quite different from that which is taught in most Christian churches today. We are

---

[13] Ephesians 6:17.

told that true spiritual warfare is hand-to-hand combat with demons, casting spells, praying certain prayers, and taking territory from Satan. *True spiritual warfare is not a battle for territory but a battle for truth.*

Ironically, while the modern church seems preoccupied with battling demons, it has developed complete apathy toward the truth. The modern church's reckless disregard for truth has handicapped its ability to wage real spiritual warfare. The church has laid aside its one God-given weapon in favor of fleshly man-made weapons which can never tear down the mental fortresses in which men are held captive.

It is not uncommon to turn on Christian TV or radio and hear Satan being bound, rebuked, and exorcised. Churches host 24-hour prayer vigils and practice spiritual mapping. "Deliverance Ministries" abound, and yet what is the state of the church?

Most churches are filled with "Christians" who cannot articulate the gospel to save their life. They tolerate false teachers by the dozens and support their ministries. The modern church has lost its ability and even willingness to discern truth from error. Churches are not interested in standing for the truth or preaching and teaching the truth. We are told that truth divides and needlessly offends people. Instead we should focus on unity, love, purpose, and more positive things. Tough subjects like sin, hell, wrath, judgment, repentance and the righteousness of God are not only neglected but avoided entirely.

Could Satan be more pleased with the modern fascination of the church? I doubt it. You can bind Satan all day long. He doesn't care, just so long as you do not share the gospel, stand for truth, or assault the errors and lies of his strongholds. You can rebuke him until you are blue in the face and he will go right along deceiving multitudes. He doesn't care, just so long as your love and focus is not the truth, sound doctrine, and preaching the gospel! Binding Satan and rebuking Satan are completely useless practices that accomplish absolutely nothing. They are unbiblical practices, manufactured in the minds of men for a church that has abandoned its call to be the "pillar and support of the truth" (1 Timothy 3:15).

Satan loves a church full of people ignorant of the gospel, who are apathetic about its defense. He thrives in churches where the lines between right and wrong, truth and error are blurred and ignored. He rejoices when he hears church leaders say that we should not concern ourselves with issues of truth and doctrine. He delights in "Christians" who think that truth should be sacrificed for the sake of unity and love. He loves "Christians" who are ignorant of the truth, for those are the most ineffective warriors of all.

So what is spiritual warfare? How do we define it? Is it exorcisms, deliverance ministries, confessing the sins of your ancestors, and renouncing generational curses? Is it rebuking Satan, binding Satan, and casting demons into pits? Is it praying down territorial spirits and claiming places and persons for God in the blood of Christ? No! No! A thousand times no!

Spiritual warfare is the bold proclamation of the truth of the gospel to lost sinners. The gospel, and the gospel alone, is powerful in God unto salvation. The gospel destroys the anti-God fortresses composed of Satan's lies. It delivers them from the kingdom of darkness and the dominion of Satan. We must proclaim and defend the truth "to open their eyes so that they may turn from darkness to light and from the dominion of Satan to God, that they may receive forgiveness of sins and an inheritance among those who have been sanctified by faith" in Christ (Acts 26:18). Spiritual warfare is a battle over truth, not territory. It is not hand-to-hand combat with demons, but the proclamation and defense of the truth of God.

We are in the business of setting men free by making them captives of Christ. We use the only divinely powerful weapon in our arsenal which is the truth of the gospel and we proclaim it boldly and watch the strongholds crumble. We proclaim, preach, teach, stand for and defend the truth so that the proud, unregenerate, sinful man will see his isms, arguments, rationalizations, and worldly-wise philosophies come crumbling down around him. He is left without excuse, naked before the truth of God and God's Word. Satan's lies are exposed and destroyed by the truth. This is true spiritual warfare - a battle of truth!

Now go out and fight the good fight!

3

The Enemy and His Army

One of the first commandments of warfare is "Know Thy Enemy." This certainly applies in the arena of spiritual warfare. We cannot afford to be ignorant of Satan's devices (2 Corinthians 2:11). Our ignorance of him and his methods only makes his job easier. Scripture reveals a tremendous amount of information about Satan and his demonic horde, in order that we might know who our enemy is, how he works, and how we can stand strong against his schemes.

It is never pleasant to spend time discussing the devil. I get no joy out of giving him any press time at all. Though this may be unpleasant, it is necessary. We need to have a theology of Satan in order that we might be kept from two opposite and equally dangerous extremes.

First, many people ignore or disbelieve his existence. Satan is portrayed in our culture as nothing more than a myth, a legend, a debunked unscientific notion of a bygone superstitious era. He is caricatured as a fiendish little man-like figure in a red suit with a cape, tail, and pitchfork. The world is not alone in its ignorance concerning the devil; his existence and reality are largely denied even in the church.

A recent Barna survey of over 1,800 "self-described Christians" found that "four out of ten strongly agree that Satan is 'not a living being but is a symbol of evil.' An additional two out of ten said they 'agree somewhat' with that perspective."[1] In other words, 60% of "Christians" think that Satan is only a symbol for evil and not a real living being. No wonder the church is falling victim to his every ploy

---

[1] http://www.barna.org/barna-update/article/12-faithspirituality/260-most-american-christians-do-not-believe-that-satan-or-the-holy-spirit-exis

and deception. Most of those in the church don't even believe they have a real enemy!

Second, many people become preoccupied with Satan and his powers. There are many who fall into the ditch of not only believing he exists, but of attributing to him far more power, influence, and ability than he really has. They see a demon behind every bush, under ever rock, and behind every event. Many Christians live in constant fear and unending terror of Satan and his demons. They fear touching something, walking by something, or saying something which will give the devil a foothold and influence in their lives. Their constant preoccupation with the demonic shifts their focus from victory in Christ to their own victimization at the hands of evil forces.

Our ability to stand against the forces of wickedness in heavenly places requires that we know our enemy and understand his methods. In this chapter we will cover a very brief theology of Satan in order that we might avoid both extremes.

A Brief History of the Devil

The Bible contains numerous references to Satan and he is called by a number of different names. He is referred to in seven books of the Old Testament. Every writer of the New Testament mentions Satan. In the gospels alone he is mentioned twenty-nine times. Twenty-five of those twenty-nine mentions are by Jesus.[2]

Satan appears very early in human history (Genesis 3), to our first parents in the garden. When writing Genesis, Moses did not explain how or why the devil existed, nor does he explain what made him evil. Moses actually assumes that his readers already believe in Satan. The final reference to Satan in the Bible foretells his doom. "And the devil who deceived them was thrown into the lake of fire and brimstone, where the beast and the false prophet are also; and they will be tormented day and night forever and ever" (Revelation 20:10).

First, we know that Satan is a created being. Jesus Christ, the second person of the Triune God is the Creator of all things

---

[2] Robert Lightner, *Angels, Satan, and Demons* (Nashville: Word Publishing, 1998), 66.

(Colossians 1:15-16) and that includes all of the angelic host. There is only one uncreated eternal being in all of the universe and that is God. God did not create evil or create evil beings. Angels were part of God's creation which He declared to be "very good" (Genesis 1:31).

As to the time of the creation of the angels, it is difficult to be dogmatic. I believe we can safely say that it was sometime prior to the creation of the heavens and the earth. It may have been during the creation week of Genesis 1.[3] By Genesis 3, Satan had been created and had rebelled. So the fall of Satan happened sometime between the "very good" of Genesis 1:31 and the appearance of this tempter in Genesis 3:1. Exactly when angels were created and how long after the creation Satan fell, we are not told.

Second, we know that Satan is a living personal being. He has all the traits of personality. He has an intellect. He is crafty. He plans and plots and uses all his resources to oppose God. He opposes God's plans, and His people. His ability to deceive and scheme is an evidence of his intellect, reason, emotion, and will. Another evidence of his personality is his ability to communicate with others, including Jesus (Luke 4:1-12).

Satan is not just a power, a force, or a myth. He is not a legend, a symbol, or the personification of evil. He is a real being with intellect, craft, will, a plan, and an ability to carry out his plan. Personal pronouns are applied to Satan in the Bible. All these things indicate that he is a personal being. He is not a human, nor was he once a man. He is a created being - a cherub.

Third, we know that Satan is a fallen angel. He once had a position of immense importance and prominence among the angels that God created. Two Old Testament passages describe Satan's original condition and his fall from that position (Isaiah 14 and Ezekiel 28).

---

[3] God said to Job that "the morning stars sang together and all the sons of God shouted for joy" when He "laid the foundation of the earth" and when He "laid its cornerstone" (Job 38:1-7). Apparently angelic beings had already been created by the time God began the creation of the heavens and the earth.

Ezekiel 28 is addressed to the "leader of Tyre" (v. 2);[4] however, beginning in verse 12, Ezekiel addresses the "king of Tyre" and describes this person in such a way as to rule out the possibility that Ezekiel was describing a man. Whereas verses 2-10 are addressed to the actual human king, verses 11-19 describe the evil spiritual power - Satan - who energized that ruler. The verses could not be addressed to the human "prince of Tyre." They can only apply to Satan himself.

> Son of man, take up a lamentation over the king of Tyre and say to him, "Thus says the Lord God, 'You had the seal of perfection, full of wisdom and perfect in beauty. You were in Eden, the garden of God; every precious stone was your covering: the ruby, the topaz and the diamond; The beryl, the onyx and the jasper; the lapis lazuli, the turquoise and the emerald; and the gold, the workmanship of your settings and sockets, was in you. On the day that you were created they were prepared. You were the anointed cherub who covers, and I placed you there. You were on the holy mountain of God; you walked in the midst of the stones of fire. You were blameless in your ways from the day you were created until unrighteousness was found in you'" (Ezekiel 28:12-15).

Ezekiel goes on to describe Satan's fall and God's subsequent judgment upon him. Satan, the "covering cherub," was "filled with violence" and "sinned" and so he was "cast as profane from the mountain of God" (v. 16). His heart was "lifted up," and he "corrupted [his] wisdom by reason of [his] splendor" (v. 17). Those verses describe his fall.

Isaiah uses the same literary device in his prophecy against the king of Babylon (Isaiah 14:4-23) as we get a glimpse behind the king of Babylon to one who was "fallen from heaven," the "star of the morning, son of the dawn" who had "weakened the nations" (v. 12). This describes Satan who said in his heart, "I will ascend to Heaven; I will raise my throne above the stars of God, and I will sit on the

---

[4] The "leader of Tyre" or "prince of Tyre" was at that time Ethbaal III who ruled the entire Phoenician seacoast city of Tyre.

mount of assembly in the recesses of the north. I will ascend above the heights of the clouds; I will make myself like the Most High" (vv. 13-14; cf. Genesis 3:15).

Satan once lived in the courts of God as one of God's cherub angels. He was a beautiful, brilliant, lovely, glorious angel - until unrighteousness was found in him. Pride was his downfall, and Satan was cast from Heaven, probably to the newly created earth.[5]

Fourth, we know a lot about Satan from the names that Scripture gives him. The name "Satan" means "adversary," and shows his true character as the one who opposes God and His plans and purposes.

He is also called "devil." That is the second most common name for Satan. "Devil" is the translation of the Greek *diabolos (διάβολος)* which means "one who engages in slander – slanderer."[6] This describes his activity as one who hurls accusations and slanders and tears down God and His people. 1 Peter 5:8 calls him "the devil, [who] prowls around like a roaring lion, seeking someone to devour."

He is also called the "serpent" since, in his temptation of Eve, he used a serpent (Genesis 3:1-6). This name speaks of his craftiness, subtlety, and beguiling nature.

His power and scope of influence are described when he is called "the prince of the power of the air" (Ephesians 2:2). His temporary control of this present world system is in view when he is called the "god of this world" (2 Corinthians 4:4). As the god of this world, Satan is busy blinding unbelievers to the truth. As a result, the "whole world lies under the power of the evil one" (1 John 5:19) during "this present evil age" (Galatians 1:4).

A large part of his work is in view when he is called "the tempter" (1 Thessalonians 3:5). The devastating destruction of his ways explains why he is called "the dragon" (Revelation 12:3-4, 7, 9, 13, 16-17).

---

[5] The philosophical problem of how a perfect angel could sin and thus fall from perfection is not without a solution. We won't address that at this time as it is beyond the scope of this chapter.

[6] J.P. & Nida Louw, E. A., *Vol. 1: Greek-English lexicon of the New Testament: Based on semantic domains* (electronic ed. of the 2nd edition) (New York: United Bible Societies, 1996), 433.

Finally, he is called "the evil one" (John 17:15; 1 John 5:18-19), and the "father of lies" (John 8:44). Those are just a few of his names. They describe not just his works, but they are indicative of his character.

We Are Not Ignorant of His Schemes

Not only does Scripture reveal much about Satan's creation and character, but it informs us of his contrivances. He is a schemer. Satan opposes everything that God does. Even if it might mean his eventual downfall and destruction (and it certainly does), He seeks to thwart all the plans and purposes of God.

We know something of his ways since we are not to be "ignorant of his schemes" (2 Corinthians 2:11) in order that we might "stand firm against the schemes of the devil" (Ephesians 6:11). One of the downfalls of many Christians is their total ignorance of Satan's schemes and tricks. However, when we look to Scripture we see all we need to know about Satan's operations and his goals.

Satan tempts people to sin and turn away from God (Matthew 4:3; 1 Thessalonians 3:5). Satan energizes and promotes every false religion in the world. All idol worship and false religion is a sacrifice to, and worship of, demons (1 Corinthians 10:20). He is the author of all deception and falsehood. With the help of his servants (2 Corinthians 11:15). He inspires false teachers (1 John 4:1-4; 1 Timothy 4:1-3) and promotes his soul-decaying error under the banner of truth and light (2 Corinthians 11:14-15).

He loves to falsely accuse Christians and to deceive people into believing those false accusations. He loves to divide the church, sow disunity, and destroy peace. He splits up families, causes strife between brethren, and undermines unity in the church and in families. These are the works of Satan.

All anti-God, worldly thinking is satanically inspired. The whole world lies under his power (1 John 5:18-19) and the whole world system is his creation (1 John 2:15-17). Every way of thinking that is opposed to God, every philosophy, every false doctrine, every lie, every worldview, religion, and thought which is raised up against the truth of God is from Satan (2 Corinthians 10:3-5). All those who promote, defend, and believe his lies have fallen prey to him and are either knowingly or unwittingly doing his bidding.

He does not present his lies and deceptions in any truthful manner. He makes sin look alluring, when in fact it is a soul-rotting poison. He tricks men into thinking that they can steal a pleasure and never pay the debt. He appears as an angel of light. He disguises error as truth and makes it sound like truth, look like truth, and feel like truth. He hides the darkness and deceives people into thinking they are walking in light when they are walking in complete spiritual darkness.

He is amazingly effective at making lies believable, sin desirable, temptation unavoidable, and error irresistible. He is so effective that the only hope we have of being able to spot his lies is to be intimately familiar with the truth. We must be so well versed in the truth, so faithful to the truth, and such a doer of truth that he will not be able to deceive us with his lies. Apart from the word of God, we are sitting ducks!

His Army

We have looked at Satan's creation, his character, and his contrivances. Scripture also tells us of his company.

Satan does not work alone. He has a host of evil spirits who are allied with him in his evil purposes. Satan is the ruler of demons (Matthew 12:22) and they do his bidding. They are united with him in his opposition to God and His people. Scripture indicates that these demons sinned at the same time that Satan did. They joined him in his rebellion and will join him in his doom. Jesus spoke of "the eternal fire [which] has been prepared for the devil and his angels" (Matthew 25:41). Revelation 12:4 refers to the fall of Satan and indicates that he took one-third of the angelic hosts with him.[7]

The other demons were originally created perfect by God and likewise fell. They, like Satan, are living, real, personal beings. They are active in the world today, involved in the same demonic activities

---

[7] John MacArthur, *The MacArthur New Testament Commentary: Revelation 12-22* (Chicago: Moody Press, 2000), 7-8.

that we attributed to Satan earlier. In Scripture, they are called "unclean spirits" (Matthew 10:1), "demons" (Matthew 12:24), and "evil spirits" (Luke 7:21).

Much of Jesus' ministry involved delivering demoniacs from their demon possession.[8] Those who were possessed by demons demonstrated unusual strength (Mark 5:1-5; Acts 19:13-16). It seems that in the New Testament demons had the ability to inflict various diseases and mental derangements upon their victims. Robert Lightner notes,

> They inflicted various diseases on people, such as dumbness (Matthew 9:33), blindness (Matthew 12:22), a form of epilepsy (Matthew 17:15-18), and mental derangement (Mark 5:1-20). Do demons do these things today? The Bible does not answer this question, but it would seem that they could and probably sometimes do. However, not all physical and mental illnesses are the results of demonic activity. Even in the New Testament times the two were distinct (Matthew 4:24; Luke 7:21).[9]

His Limitations

In God's Word we learn of Satan's creation, character, contrivances, company and also his constraints.

All I have written to this point would probably cause panic, terror, sleepless nights and anxiety attacks. But this is not the full story. No treatment of Satan and his demons would be complete without also learning of their limitations.

First, demons are greater than man in knowledge but they are not omniscient.[10] Angels are considered to have great wisdom (2 Samuel 14:20) and knowledge (Matthew 24:36). Even fallen angels have knowledge beyond the natural realm (Luke 4:34). Yet they are not omniscient beings. Only God is omniscient.

---

[8] We will examine this practice in Chapter 12.

[9] Lightner, 92.

[10] This summary of the limitations of demons is borrowed from Henry C. Thiessen, *Lectures in Systematic Theology* (Grand Rapids: Eerdman's Publishing Company, 1949), 134-135.

Second, though demons are stronger than men, they are not omnipotent. Angels are said to be greater in power and might (2 Peter 2:11; Psalm 103:20). They are called "mighty angels." Demons in their fallen state still retained that strength and superiority over men (Acts 19:13-16), though they are not almighty. Only God is omnipotent.

Third, though demons are more mobile than man, they are not omnipresent. They have to roam and walk about on the earth (Job 1:7; Zechariah 1:11; 1 Peter 5:8). Angels have to move and sometimes there are even delays because of their inability to instantly transport themselves (Daniel 10:10-14). Satan cannot be in more than one place at any given time. Only God is omnipresent.

An important limitation on Satan's power is seen in Job 1-2. Satan was unable to touch anything that Job owned, or to afflict Job in any way because God had placed "a hedge around him and his house and all that he has, on every side" (Job 1:10). Satan had to receive permission from God before He could touch Job's possessions (Job 1:12) or his health (Job 2:6).

We can take comfort in the fact that Satan can do nothing unless God, by His sovereign hand, for His sovereign purposes, and in accordance with His secret will allows it! Satan can only do what God gives him the freedom to do. He cannot do anything at any time to anybody, anywhere without God's permission. Satan is like a dog on his master's leash. God allows him to go so far and no further, to do so much and no more.

God is allowing Satan to work his plan with a certain degree of freedom. I believe that God restrains more of his evil than He allows. God is sovereign over all things, and that includes Satan and his demons, their evil schemes, and their activities.

Satan is not as powerful as God, and God is not "trying" to defeat Him. Satan is a crushed and defeated foe whose doom is certain. Ultimately, Satan's doom was secured the instant he fell in prideful rebellion, since it is impossible that God should fall from His throne or that His plans and purposes fail.

Satan's end and destruction was publicly secured on the cross where Jesus "disarmed the rulers and authorities, He made a public display of them, having triumphed over them" (Colossians 2:15).

Jesus, through death, rendered "powerless him who had the power of death, that is the devil" (Hebrews 2:14-15). 1 John 3:8 says that "the Son of God appeared for this purpose, to destroy the works of the devil." He has certainly done so. The ruler of this world has been judged (John 16:11).

The Christian's Response

What then should be our response?

Do you remember the two extremes we need to avoid? To ignore Satan, disbelieve his existence, and not at all be concerned with his schemes is to be blinded to a very real and very dangerous enemy. To be fixated on Satan and preoccupied with Him is to give far too much attention to an already defeated foe. There is certainly a balanced, middle-ground approach.

In order to avoid the first error, we must be alert. We have to know our enemy, his tactics and his limitations. We need to be wise to his schemes of division, deception and destruction. We need to be able to identify satanic attacks and stand against them. We need to be able to discern the difference between truth and error, right and wrong. We need to keep our heads up and stay engaged in the game. A certain degree of wariness is appropriate. We must walk circumspectly, knowing the times and discerning truth.

In order to avoid the second error, we must be firm. We have to rest in the victory, the armor, and the safety secured for us. Christ has won the victory. Satan is limited. He is active, but he is defeated. The "check mate" has been secured and now it is only a matter of time and a few moves and the Victor will appear and put down all His enemies.

We are in Christ and cannot be snatched away by Satan (John 10:25-30). Our salvation is secure. Our victory over death and every enemy has been secured by Christ and affirmed in His resurrection (1 Corinthians 15:50-58). We have the spiritual armor necessary to stand against the wiles of the devil (Ephesians 6:10-17). Christ has provided all we need - we must stand therein!

An understanding of the Bible's teaching on Satan and his demons will keep us from falling to his temptations and attacks and from constantly living in fear of him. Be alert. Be firm in your faith.

4

The World and the Flesh

After the last chapter, you may be hoping that our discussion of the forces allied against us is over. It is daunt to think that Satan and all his vast army is entrenched in their opposition to us. The last thing we want to hear is that Satan and his demons are not our only enemy, but the truth is, we have two more!

When most people hear the words "spiritual warfare" they envision some sort of cosmic battle between angels or between men and demons. The focus is typically on Satan and his demons. When asked to name the Christian's enemy, most would unhesitatingly answer, "The devil and his demons." Though that answer is true, it is not complete. We actually have three enemies, not one.

Our study of the subject of spiritual warfare would be inadequate if it failed to account for all three enemies. We have taken the time to understand the powers and restrictions, and the abilities and inabilities of the devil in the previous chapter. Now we will turn our attention to the other two enemies we fight: the *world* and the *flesh*.

The Danger of Ignoring the Enemy

One thing I enjoy doing with my children is wrestling. We writhe around on the floor in the front room while I taunt and tickle and do everything in my power to not let any of them escape my clutches. They scream and laugh and try their best to fight back. When the kids were smaller, I could take on all four of them at once without a problem. That is no longer the case!

Occasionally, I would notice that one or two of the kids would stand off to the side, waiting for the perfect opportunity to attack.

They wisely stayed just out of arms' reach, keeping their distance, and patiently waiting. I soon found that all I had to do to invite an attack was to turn my back to the waiting child. By focusing all my attention on one of the other kids, those waiting in the wings sensed a weakness, a blind spot, and thus, their opportunity. They would quickly move in for the attack and try to get the upper hand.

This same scenario gets played out in the arena of spiritual warfare. Spiritual warfare is not a battle waged against one single enemy. It is a battle we wage against three separate enemies who all work in concert against the Christian.

If our focus is on only one of the three enemies, we will quickly find that we are losing the battle on the other two fronts. Too often, attention is focused on the devil and defeating him while the battle against the world and the flesh is neglected. "As a result of being so preoccupied with only one phase of the battle, many Christians have suffered great infiltration on the fronts of the world and the flesh."[1]

We see the results of being preoccupied with the demonic in the church today. A quick search for resources on spiritual warfare will turn up no lack of material. Deliverance ministries, study resources, books, and tapes abound. Never in the history of the church has so much material been available to *supposedly* equip us for battling spiritual forces.

At the same time, it is obvious that the church is losing its battle against the world and the flesh. Worldliness has not only infiltrated the church, in most sectors, it has entirely taken over. A love for all things temporal, an infatuation with relevance, and an embrace of modern culture has handicapped the Church. Pastors and ministry leaders crave acceptance in academia and political circles. The average Sunday morning at your local "seeker driven church" feels more like a buffet of pop culture than a feast on God's Word. Worldly thinking and man-centered theology are the driving forces behind nearly all church growth methodologies. Consequently, these worldly churches think that evangelism entails pandering to the

---

[1] Thomas Ice and Robert Dean, Jr., *Overrun By Demons: The Church's New Preoccupation With The Demonic* (Eugene: Harvest House Publishers, 1990), 61.

desires of unbelievers and crafting a message that does not confront their worldly thinking.

How are Christians doing in battling against the flesh? Are we beating that enemy? Hardly. Statistics show that *professing* Christians are just as likely to lie, steal, divorce, view pornography, gossip, and cheat on their taxes as their pagan counterparts. Disunity, pride, self-centeredness, greed, and discontentment are not traits exclusively found among unbelievers. They have become firmly entrenched in the modern church. Doesn't this seem a bit incongruous?

Though many factors could account for this, we certainly cannot deny the fact that while seeking to do battle with Satan and his demons, most Christians have turned their back on the other two enemies. Consequently, the world and the flesh are winning victory after victory in the lives of believers. We may be fighting with all our might and standing strong against the wiles of the devil, but if we have adopted the godless thinking that characterizes the world while constantly living in the flesh, what is the point?

Only a balanced warfare against all three enemies simultaneously will ensure our victory. Let's familiarize ourselves with our other two enemies.

THE WORLD

By *"the world,"* I do not mean, and Scripture does not mean, all the individual people in the world. We are not speaking of "the world" in the sense of every person on the planet.

By *"the world"* we mean the system of thinking, the way of life, the perspective of this world which leaves no room for God. It is the godless mindset composed of the "lust of the flesh," "the lust of the eyes," and the "boastful pride of life" (1 John 2:15-17).

You have probably heard people refer to "worldly Christians." Usually such a label is associated with certain activities such as smoking, going to movies, listening to certain styles of music, playing cards, drinking a glass of wine or watching football on Sundays. The biblical concept of worldliness has less to do with certain activities and more to do with certain ways of thinking. Sexual immorality, drunkenness, revelry and the like are sins of the flesh and are not worldliness, per se. These things may be encouraged or justified by worldly thinking and the world system, but they are deeds of the flesh.

Worldliness is a way of thinking, an overall philosophy of life, which stirs the flesh to indulge in specific sins. It is a mindset and a worldview, a systematic approach to life which leaves no room for God and His Word. It is a way of thinking that is humanistic, man-centered, and self-sufficient.

Lewis Sperry Chafer described the world system, writing:
The cosmos [meaning "world"] is a vast order or system that Satan has promoted which conforms us to his ideals, aims, and methods. It is civilization now functioning apart from God - a civilization which none of its promoters really expect God to share, who assign to God no consideration in respect to their projects. This system embraces its godless governments, conflicts, armaments, and jealousies, [as well as] its education, culture, religions of morality, and pride. It is that sphere in which man lives. It is what he sees, what he employs. To the uncounted multitude it is all they ever know so long as they live on this earth. It is properly styled "the satanic system," which phrase is in many instances a justified interpretation of the so meaningful word "cosmos." It is literally a cosmos diabolicus.[2]

Whenever we think like the world, we are thinking exactly the way that Satan wants us to! We are told,
Do not love the world nor the things in the world. If anyone loves the world, the love of the Father is not in him. For all that is in the world, the lust of the flesh and the lust of the eyes and the boastful pride of life, is not from the Father, but is from the world. The world is passing away, and also its lusts; but the one who does the will of God lives forever (1 John 2:15-17).

---

[2] Lewis Sperry Chafer, *Systematic Theology, Vol. II* (Dallas Seminary Press, 1948), 77. Quoted by Ice and Dean in *Overrun By Demons*, 60-61.

James 1:27 says that "pure and undefiled religion in the sight of our God and Father is this: to visit orphans and widows in their distress, and to keep oneself unstained by the world." James rebuked those who fraternize with this enemy saying, "You adulteresses, do you not know that friendship with the world is hostility toward God? Therefore whoever wishes to be a friend of the world makes himself an enemy of God" (James 4:4). The wisdom that is of this world "is not that which comes down from above, but is earthly, natural, demonic" (James 3:15).

Christians are hated by the world because we are not of this world (1 John 3:1, 13). We should not love this world, but instead overcome it (1 John 4:4; 5:4) since the whole world system "lies in the power of the evil one" (1 John 5:19).

Winning against the World

The oft-heard slogan in Christian circles is true: "Believers are in the world, but not of the world." Believers do not belong to this world because we have been chosen out of the world. "If you were of the world, the world would love its own; but because you are not of the world, but I chose you out of the world, because of this the world hates you" (John 15:19). Having been born of God, the evil one cannot touch us (1 John 5:18-19) because we have been delivered from the domain of darkness and transferred to the kingdom of His beloved Son (Colossians 1:13).

What then is our relationship to this world? Though we are not of this world (John 17:14, 16), we do live in this world (John 17:15). We are left in this world to evangelize it while we remain separate from it.

A number of New Testament passages speak of our separation from the world in our lifestyle and behavior. "Do not be conformed to this world, but be transformed by the renewing of your mind, so that you may prove what the will of God is, that which is good and acceptable and perfect" (Romans 12:2). The grace of God instructs us to "deny ungodliness and worldly desires and to live sensibly, righteously and godly in the present age, looking for the blessed hope and the appearing of the glory of our great God and Savior,

Christ Jesus" (Titus 2:12-13). We are to "keep oneself unstained by the world" (James 1:27), and never wish or seek friendship with the world (James 4:4). We have "escaped the corruption that is in the world by lust" (2 Peter 1:4) and "have escaped the defilements of the world by the knowledge of the Lord and Savior Jesus Christ, . . ." (2 Peter 2:20).

When you "let your light shine before men in such a way that they may see your good works, and glorify your Father who is in Heaven" (Matthew 5:16), then "you will prove yourselves to be blameless and innocent, children of God above reproach in the midst of a crooked and perverse generation, among whom you appear as lights in the world, holding fast the word of life" (Philippians 2:15-16).

We separate from the world when we live and think differently from the godless system which permeates every corner of human thinking, culture, and conduct. Jesus was our model of how to live in the world while confronting the world system.

> Christ bore witness to the sinfulness of the world's conduct by demonstrating the moral perfection of God in His life; so also, by allowing the holy character of God to radiate in his life, the believer exposes the sinfulness of the world's practices, showing that they are contrary to God's holy character. Christ also bore witness to the truth by showing men who God is and what He requires of them; so also, the believer bears witness to the truth, relating the life, death, and resurrection of the Lord Jesus. In these two ways the believer fulfills his responsibility of being a witness to the world.[3]

We wage war on the world system by standing against its godless philosophies, speculations, and lofty, self-reliant thinking. We proclaim the truth, bringing every thought of the unbeliever captive to the obedience of Christ (2 Corinthians 10:3-5). The degree to which believers individually, or the church corporately, begins to

---

[3] Allan S. Maitha, *The World: Enemy of the Believer* (Th.M. Thesis from Dallas Seminary, 1970) as quoted in *Overrun By Demons*, pg. 73.

adopt the world's thinking on marriage, ministry, truth, and all aspects of life and living is the degree to which they lose the spiritual battle.

Satan does not have to possess you in order to get you to do his will. He does not have to oppress, control or personally attack you. All he has to do is to get you to think and act like the world, and you are doing his will. Scary, isn't it?

THE FLESH

On June 29, 2010, a CBS headline read, "FBI: 10 Russian Spies Arrested in U.S." Posing as innocent civilians in New York, Washington, and Boston, these ten Russian agents sought to infiltrate U.S. policy-making circles to gather intelligence about U.S. weapons, diplomatic strategy and political developments.[4]

According to the news story, "These deep-cover agents are the hardest spies for the FBI to catch and are dubbed 'illegals' in the intelligence world because they take civilian jobs with no visible connection to a foreign government, rather than operating from government jobs inside Russian embassies and military missions."[5]

Few threats are feared as much as "the traitor" - a rebel within the camp. They work covertly to overthrow the government and subvert its interests. They can be far more effective than outside threats.

Just as nations have their traitors, spies, and rebels within the camp, so does the Christian have theirs - the flesh. The other two enemies that we face - Satan and the world - are both *external* enemies. Neither one of those enemies has the power to make any person disobey God. That which gives Satan and the world-system the opportunity to operate in the believer's life is the flesh.

Where Did It Come From?

"Flesh" is the word that the New Testament most often uses to describe the sin nature which is the ruling principle within all the

---

[4] http://www.cbsnews.com/stories/2010/06/28/world/main6627393.shtml posted online as of October 26, 2010.

[5] Ibid.

fallen children of Adam. The moment that Adam sinned in the garden, he acquired a sin nature. It is a principle, an influence, a disposition to sin which completely rules the unbeliever. It is the desire to assert one's own will and authority over God in every area of life. It is passed on, at conception, to all of Adam's descendants.

Romans 8 is a key passage on the nature, extent, and influence of the sinful nature - the flesh. All who are in Adam are in the flesh and controlled by the flesh. Thus they "cannot please God" because they are "hostile toward God" and are not "subject to the law of God" (Romans 8:1-17). Apart from the new birth, the unbeliever has no new nature, no spiritual capacity to do anything pleasing to God. They are slaves of sin (John 8:34).

The flesh produces a wide range of sins and sinful activities (Galatians 5:19-21). It also produces what, on the surface, appears to be good deeds and righteous acts. None were more outwardly righteous than Saul of Tarsus (Philippians 3:2-6) and yet all his righteous activities were sinful because he was seeking to establish his own righteousness apart from Christ (Philippians 3:7-11). What is it that prompts someone to do religious activities in an effort to gain God's favor? The flesh. The flesh in its pride seeks to establish itself and its own efforts as meritorious before God.

Our Main Enemy

The clear teaching of the New Testament is that the flesh, not the devil, is the major and most influential enemy that the Christian faces.[6] The world is *not* our most powerful and influential enemy. The devil is *not* our most powerful and influential enemy. The *flesh is* our most powerful and influential enemy!

As Ice and Dean accurately point out,

The 21 letters in the New Testament were written to address the important issues confronting Christians in this age, the church age. It is reasonable to expect that if anything is an important issue for the believer in this age it will be given a comprehensive treatment in these letters,

---

[6] Romans 7:14, 18; 8:1-17; Galatians 3:3; 5:13-21; Ephesians 2:3.

and that if something isn't an issue it will probably be ignored.

The silence of these letters in some areas speaks volumes. For example, demons (or evil spirits) are mentioned only ten times, and most of these simply relate to certain factual truths about demons. . . . On the other hand, in these same letters are over 50 references to the flesh as the primary enemy of the Christian (and "the flesh" is only one way that this sin nature is referred to). It is obvious that the New Testament perspective is that the major area of conflict is in the arena of the flesh.[7]

To quote one of my Bible College friends, "Satan doesn't need to tempt me to sin or make me to sin. My flesh is more than capable of causing my downfall." Yet, the bulk of spiritual warfare teaching today is aimed at conquering Satan - an already defeated foe.

Winning against the Flesh

Though we once were slaves of sin and in bondage to the flesh, salvation has delivered us from the power of that sinful nature. Romans 6:17-18 says, "But thanks be to God that though you were slaves of sin, you became obedient from the heart to that form of teaching to which you were committed, and having been freed from sin, you became slaves of righteousness."

Since we have been identified with Christ in His death, burial, and resurrection, our "old man" is crucified, dead, and gone. We are no longer the person we once were in Adam. We are now new creatures in Christ (2 Corinthians 5:17).[8] Though our old man (our identity in Adam) is dead and gone, the sin nature continues. We still have to battle against the flesh. This is what leads to the struggle that Paul describes in Romans 7 where we do the deeds we don't want to and do not do what we want to do. Though I am no longer "in Adam," and though I have been set free from the power of sin, there still

---

[7] Ice, pg. 76-77.
[8] The "old man" refers to the person we once were in Adam before being saved: Ephesians 4:22, 24; Romans 6:6; Colossians 3:9-10.

dwells within me a sinful nature, the flesh which wars against the Spirit (Galatians 5:16-24).

How are we to deal with this propensity toward sin, the flesh? Romans 6 is key. First, we are to *know* that our old self was crucified with Christ and we are no longer slaves of sin (vv. 1-10). Second, we are to *consider* ourselves to be free from sin, dead to sin (v. 11), and not let sin reign in our body by obeying it in its lusts (v. 12). We must believe that sin no longer has power over us and then live in light of that fact. We accept by faith, believing it true, that we are no longer slaves to sin. Third, we choose obedience and obey God and His Word. In this way, we walk by faith believing what Scripture says about our emancipation from sin.

Victory over sin comes down to choosing to obey righteousness. If we present ourselves as slaves of righteousness and choose to do righteousness, then in obeying righteousness we become slaves of righteousness. If we choose to yield our bodies to sin, then we will becomes slaves to sin. The unalterable law of sanctification is that we become slaves to the one whom we obey (Romans 6:16). Romans 6:19 says, "For just as you presented your members as slaves to impurity and to lawlessness, resulting in further lawlessness, so now present your members as slaves to righteousness, resulting in sanctification."

We are engaged in a step-by-step, day-by-day, decision-by-decision walk with Christ. Our sin nature has power over us only if we choose to obey it. We are engaged in a lifelong, daily, habitual battle against the flesh. The Spirit wages war against the flesh and the flesh against the Spirit (Galatians 5:17) for as the Apostle Peter reminds us, the fleshly lusts wage war against our soul (1 Peter 2:11).

The Christian life is not lived on some mystical plane, free of this daily battle. We live our lives shackled to this body of death, this sinful flesh, and we long for the deliverance that will come either at death or the Lord's return (Romans 7:24-25; 8:18-25).

The Puritans used to use a phrase that has unfortunately fallen into disuse: the mortification of sin. We kill sin. It is our enemy. We fight the fight, wage the war. We put to death the deeds of the flesh (Romans 8:13), resisting temptation, choosing obedience, waging war against the enemy within, by the grace and strength of Christ.

56

The Enemies Unite

We have three enemies - the world, the flesh, and the devil. These three work in concert with each other against the believer. To give you some idea of how they work together, consider the following illustration offered by Ice and Dean in their book, *Overrun By Demons*:

> All unbelievers are in bondage to Satan, making them his unwitting allies against God. He makes them dance in harmony to the tune of the world-system.
>
> This system operates similar to the way a radio station functions. Satan is the program director who selects the agenda for the station. The demons and fallen humanity produce the programming, which propagates and reinforces the agenda (false doctrine). The station then transmits the message over the air. However, you cannot pick up the station unless you have a receiver tuned to the right frequency. Fallen humanity is all tuned in to the radio station "WORLD" with the volume turned all the way up. The receiver is the flesh, which is attracted to Satan's frequency. All three work in harmony: the world, the flesh, and the devil.
>
> The unbeliever's nature is sympathetic to the evil nature of the world-system, so the two are attracted. The main difference between the two is that the world-system characterizes the corporate expression of Satan while the flesh embodies these same characteristics on a personal level. When an individual becomes a believer in Jesus Christ this alignment is broken and all-out war begins between the Christian and the world.[9]

---

[9] Ice and Dean, 69-70.

Part 2:
Exposing Unbiblical
Practices

5

<u>Carnal Weapons: Hedges</u>

It is time to turn a bit of a corner. The material we have covered so far has served to build a biblical framework by which we can evaluate certain practices. We have laid a foundation upon which a biblical theology of spiritual warfare can be built.

We have affirmed that the Bible and the Bible alone should govern our theology of spiritual warfare (Chapter 1). We have seen from 2 Corinthians 10 that spiritual warfare is not a hand-to-hand battle with demons over territory, but a battle over truth waged with the Word of God (Chapter 2). We have spent some time considering our three enemies, and how they work in concert with one another (Chapters 3 & 4).

In the next few chapters, we will evaluate certain practices which are often associated with spiritual warfare. These practices are assumed by many to be biblical. The language of certain spiritual warfare techniques has made its way into the Christian vernacular, and well-intentioned believers have adopted these methods, often without ever pausing to evaluate them in the light of Scripture.

Why Bother?

Imagine a soldier on the front lines who ignored the commands of his superior and chose to prosecute a battle according to his own designs. The soldier may think that his method of fighting the enemy is better or more effective than his commander's. He might believe that what he has practiced for so many years could not possibly be wrong. No matter his motives, to fail to follow the orders of his commander, and to go outside the boundaries set by his superior, is gross insubordination and disobedience to clear commands.

We have a Commander-In-Chief who has described our warfare, commissioned us, and equipped us to fight. If He has given orders as to how this battle for the truth is to be waged, then we are negligent at best and disobedient at worst to ignore His instruction and adopt methodologies that He has not sanctioned nor commanded.

Our Superior is no mere fallible human. He is infallible and omniscient. To engage in spiritual warfare practices which He has neither commanded nor approved is disobedience, insubordination, and outright foolishness. Why would we want to fight such a powerful enemy using carnal, fleshly weapons of man's making? Why would we want to live and battle in our own strength? To do so is to invite disaster.[1]

It is necessary that we evaluate certain practices which have crept in to the modern understanding of spiritual warfare. Some of the things we are going to be discussing might be things you have read about, seen and heard others do, or even done yourself. I contend that well-intentioned people have taught a lot of spurious things concerning spiritual warfare. Some have become such a part of the warp and woof of modern American evangelicalism as to make questioning them an act of treason! Yet question we must.

We have a responsibility to evaluate our thinking and behavior in light of Scripture and seek to conform our lives to God's Word. If what we have been taught concerning spiritual warfare is not founded upon the text of Scripture, we should be quick to abandon it, however dear the practice may be or however effective we might perceive it to be. If we don't analyze the specifics of our practices in light of Scripture, then we end up plugging our "carnal weapons" into a biblical paradigm. That result is confusion and ineffective warfare.

Nothing you read in the next few chapters is intended to be hateful criticism. Please don't take it that way. Criticism can be good if it is done rightly. Our desire should always be to bring our thoughts, motives, practices and beliefs to the anvil of God's Word to pound them into conformity to His revealed truth. A necessary

---

[1] 2 Corinthians 10:3-5 tells us that our warfare is not to be waged using weapons, methods, or tactics which are of man's creation. We are not free to adopt any practice which we might invent.

corollary to teaching the truth is to identify error and offer correction. When God's people are engaged in unbiblical practices, the loving thing to do is to point it out and correct it. It is unloving to allow someone to continue in an error which will prove to be a danger to their spiritual well being.[2]

Engaging the battle with wrong methods is as bad or worse than no warfare at all. My prayer is that God's people will abandon unbiblical thinking, extra-biblical and unbiblical practices, and engage in true spiritual warfare, according to the orders and example of our Commander given to us in His Word. If we don't address erroneous practices and expose the unbiblical methodologies currently used, then we can't build a biblical methodology in its place. It is impossible to build a new building where an old, useless one currently stands. It is therefore necessary to do a little destruction on the proposed site before any construction can take place.

Woven into the Fabric

Practices such as binding Satan, praying a "hedge of thorns," renouncing generational curses, naming and praying against territorial spirits, exorcising demons from Christians, pagans, or inanimate objects, rebuking the devil, and pleading the blood of Jesus have become virtually woven into the fabric of modern notions of spiritual warfare. The legitimacy of these practices is assumed and never questioned. These have become so much a part of the fabric of the prayers and lives of some people and churches, that to question their legitimacy, in some circles, qualifies one as a "heretic."[3]

I suspect that some who are reading about these things have never, prior to reading this book, been exposed to any of this teaching or these practices. Consider yourself very fortunate! You might find it hard to believe that people actually do this, but trust me - they do.

---

[2] Jesus and the Apostles constantly confronted unbiblical practices and beliefs (Matthew 5-8; John 3, 8, 10). Whole books of the Bible were written to this very end (Galatians, 1 Corinthians, 2 Corinthians, Colossians, 1 Thessalonians, 2 Thessalonians, 1 Timothy, Titus, 2 Peter, 1 John, Jude).

[3] There was a time when I thought all of these were biblical methods of spiritual warfare. However, I believe that a careful look at Scripture reveals these practices are based upon bad interpretation and verses cited out of context.

These things are not isolated to some fringe movement within Christianity. They are taught in fundamentalist, conservative, Bible-believing, and gospel-centered churches. They are not the unique property of the charismatic movement.

I am in no way questioning the intentions of those who practice or teach the methodologies evaluated here. I only seek to evaluate the practices.

Praying the Hedge of Thorns

If you have never been exposed to this teaching before, you are probably asking yourself, "What in the world is that?!?"

Supposedly, this is the practice of erecting a "spiritual hedge" around persons, places, or things in order to prohibit satanic influence or attack. Once a "hedge of thorns" is prayed around someone, Satan and his demons can't get through. This is different from the practice of binding Satan. In binding Satan, he is kept from doing something (supposedly) that he otherwise could do. In praying the hedge of thorns, you are not taking Satan's ability away, but rather protecting someone from him. It is taught that the practice of "praying a hedge" prevents demonic/satanic influence in the life or mind of the person protected by the hedge.

The "hedge" is often treated as an all-purpose hedge. You might pray it for your spouse, your family, your home, your children, your job, your car, your church, or even your town. If you want to win unbelievers to Christ, first pray a hedge of thorns around the person so they cannot be attacked or influenced demonically.

Those who "pray a hedge" usually pray something like this, "Lord, I pray a hedge of protection around this house in Jesus' name. I pray a hedge of thorns around my kids in Jesus' name. I pray a hedge around Bob, who needs salvation. And Lord, I pray a hedge of thorns around the church service this Sunday, in Jesus' name. . ."

Apparently, praying this one time is not sufficient, for we are encouraged by experts in spiritual warfare to pray it regularly, at least daily, if not several times a day. I'm not sure if this is because the hedge breaks down over time, or if Satan is crafty enough to find a means of getting over or through the hedge. I would think that if this methodology was effective at all, it only needs to be done one time. Why can't we simply pray a hedge of protection (hedge of thorns) around everything and just prevent Satan from influencing anything at all? Better yet, why not just pray a hedge of thorns around Satan himself and all his demons? Rather than building a hedge around everything and everyone to keep the devil out, why not pray a hedge around him to keep him in? It would be a Hedge of Thorns Penitentiary for Satan.

I was first exposed to this teaching at a Basic Youth Conflicts Seminar in Spokane, Washington taught via video by Bill Gothard. He mentioned this practice and gave details on how to effectively do it. He also cited the "supporting" references of Hosea 2:6 and Job 1:10. It was not too long after that I was exposed to this teaching in a much more developed form. It sounded biblical. It made sense to me that we could prohibit Satan from influencing people or places by using this practice. When I looked up the Bible verses, they did mention a "hedge." I assumed it must be biblical.

But is that really what these passages teach? An examination of these oft-cited texts shows that biblical support for "praying the hedge" is thin indeed. Let's take a look at each of these texts in their contexts.

Hosea 2:6

"Therefore, behold, I will hedge up her way with thorns, And I will build a wall against her so that she cannot find her paths."

At first glance you'll notice a reference to "hedge" and "thorns." Some jump at that and say, "See? There it is! That is the 'hedge of thorns!'"

You don't have to be a careful student of Scripture to recognize that the mere mention of "hedge" and "thorns" in one verse is not sufficient to support the elaborate practice described above. A consideration given to the context in which this verse appears shows its true meaning and reveals that no such practice of "praying a hedge" against demonic forces is in view by Hosea. In fact, this is a perfect example of wrenching a verse from its context and using it to prop up a teaching that is completely foreign to the meaning and intention of the passage.

Punishment Not Protection

Hosea was a prophet that God called to be an unusual object lesson to the nation of Israel. God commanded Hosea to "take a wife of harlotry and have children of harlotry; for the land commits flagrant harlotry, forsaking the LORD." Hosea did this in marrying Gomer (1:2-3). Even the names given to the children of Hosea and Gomer bore prophetic significance as a sign and message to the nation (1:4-11).

This was a powerful prophetic object lesson. The practices of harlotry, adultery, and impurity are commonly used to illustrate the defiling and polluting nature of the spiritual apostasy of the nation.[4] To forsake their God by covenant and turn to other gods in idolatry was as the sin of harlotry and adultery. Hosea's marriage to Gomer and her subsequent unfaithfulness proved to be a vivid picture of God's covenant relationship with the nation of Israel and the pollution of that covenant by their persistent idolatry. Their apostasy was likened to harlotry.

It is in that context that we come to Chapter 2 of Hosea's prophecy. With that in mind, read the entire context while noticing the emphasized references to the unfaithfulness of the nation.

Hosea 2:1-13

1 "Say to your brothers, 'Ammi,' and to your sisters, 'Ruhamah.' 2 Contend with your mother, contend, For she is **not my wife**, and I am **not her husband**; And let her put away **her harlotry** from her face And **her adultery from between her breasts**, 3 Or I will **strip her naked** And **expose her** as on the day when she was born. I will also make her like a wilderness, Make her like desert land And slay her with thirst. 4 Also, I will have no compassion on her children, Because they are **children of harlotry**. 5 For

---

[4] Ezekiel 16:20, 25; 23:43.

their mother has **played the harlot**; She who conceived them has **acted shamefully**. For she said, 'I **will go after my lovers**, Who give me my bread and my water, My wool and my flax, my oil and my drink.' 6 *Therefore, behold, I will hedge up her way with thorns, And I will build a wall against her so that she cannot find her paths.* 7 She will **pursue her lovers**, but she will **not overtake them**; And she **will seek them**, but will **not find them**. Then she will say, 'I **will go back to my first husband**, For it was better for me then than now!' 8 For she does not know that it was I who gave her the grain, the new wine and the oil, And lavished on her silver and gold, Which they used for Baal. 9 Therefore, I will take back My grain at harvest time And My new wine in its season. I will also take away My wool and My flax Given to cover **her nakedness**. 10 And then I will **uncover her lewdness** In the sight of **her lovers**, And no one will rescue her out of My hand. 11 I will also put an end to all her gaiety, Her feasts, her new moons, her Sabbaths And all her festal assemblies. 12 I will destroy her vines and fig trees, Of which she said, 'These are my wages Which **my lovers have given me**.' And I will make them a forest, And the beasts of the field will devour them. 13 I will punish her for the **days of the Baals** When she used to offer sacrifices to them And **adorn herself with her earrings and jewelry**, And **follow her lovers**, so that she forgot Me," declares the Lord.

It is difficult to miss the point! Does the passage sound like it has anything to do with spiritual warfare? Does it sound like it has anything at all to do with instruction on how to prevent satanic influence, demonic oppression, or with protecting the righteous? It does not. In fact, the passage describes a *judgment*, not a *protection*! Hosea is describing a coming judgment of God upon the nation that involved "hedging them in with thorns" so that they would return to Him. The text has nothing to do with protecting God's people from

Satan. It was not done *for* His people, but *against* them. The hedge of thorns is not protection but judgment!

God was revealing that the nation was about to experience severe judgment for its spiritual harlotry. God would "hedge up her [the nation] way with thorns" and "build a wall against her [the nation - His people by covenant] so that she cannot find her paths."

What "way" was God promising to hedge with thorns? It would be the nation's idolatrous paths, their pursuit of other gods. Notice the references to pursuing their spiritual harlotry:

She said, "I will go after my lovers" (v. 5).
She will pursue her lovers, but not overtake them (v. 5).
She will seek them, but will not find them (v. 5).
She used to. . . follow her lovers (v. 13).

It is those paths of unrighteous pursuit of spiritual adultery and harlotry that God is describing through Hosea. The judgment of God upon the nation would be a path of difficulty and pain - hedged as with thorns.

The metaphor is an easy one to understand. You can imagine being on a straight and narrow path on which both sides are hedged with thorns. To turn to the right or to the left, to seek to depart from said path would only result in running into thorns - misery! In fact, that is evident in the very next verse. Hosea 2:7 says, "She will pursue her lovers, but she will not overtake them; And she will seek them, but will not find them. Then she will say, 'I will go back to my first husband, For it was better for me then than now!'"

The whole intention of God hedging in the nation from its perverse ways, was so that in experiencing the misery of spiritual harlotry, they would say, "I will go back to my first husband [God - their covenant partner]."

What types of misery [thorns] was God promising the unfaithful nation? Look at this list from the chapter:

She will be stripped naked (v. 3).
She will be exposed (v. 3).

She will be made like a wilderness (v. 3).
She will be made like a desert land (v. 3).
She will be slayed with thirst (v. 3).
God will have no compassion (v. 4).
God will withhold the provision of grain at harvest (v.9).
God will withhold the provision of wine (v. 9).
God will take away provision of wool and flax (v. 9).
God will uncover her lewdness (v. 10).
God will prevent rescue from her dire situation (v. 10).
God will put an end to her happiness (v. 11).
Festive assemblies and celebrations will end (v. 11).
God will destroy vines and fig trees (v. 12).
She will be punished for worship of Baal (v. 13).

All of those things are the thorns that would afflict God's people. God was saying, "I will bring judgment on this nation because of their harlotries with other gods. I will make these people so miserable in their sins, I will remove every blessing, and make every pursuit of idols so painful, that they will eventually return to Me."

If you told Hosea, "Oh, so we can pray this 'hedge of thorns' around our loved ones for protection from Satan and demonic influence," he would respond, "Huh?!"

Obviously such a notion is entirely foreign to the context. Yet this whole theology of spiritual warfare and a whole prayer practice is built upon the mention of "hedge" and "thorns" in the same verse without any consideration of what the verse actually teaches.

Hosea 2:6 has nothing at all to do with spiritual warfare and protection from demons. Nothing. It refers to an act of God in judgment to punish the nation and prevent them from pursuing their idolatrous lusts.

Nothing in Hosea 2 indicates that such a hedge can be created through prayer. There is nothing here that teaches that this was a result of prayer. There is no mention of Satan or how such a "hedge of thorns" prevents his activity. There is no indication that you and I can even do anything to construct such a hedge. It is not even a literal hedge. It is a metaphor for punishment not protection. It is a figure of speech, and one that has nothing at all to do with spiritual warfare.

Job 1

Doesn't the book of Job mention a hedge that protected righteous Job? Yes, in fact, a second passage pressed into service to support the practice of praying a hedge of protection is Job 1:8-10. "The Lord said to Satan, 'Have you considered My servant Job? For there is no one like him on the earth, a blameless and upright man, fearing God and turning away from evil.' Then Satan answered the Lord, 'Does Job fear God for nothing? Have You not made a hedge about him and his house and all that he has, on every side? You have blessed the work of his hands, and his possessions have increased in the land. But put forth Your hand now and touch all that he has; he will surely curse You to Your face.'"

Some would say, "See, there is a hedge mentioned there, one of protection that kept Satan from attacking Job."

That is certainly true. The text does mention a hedge and this hedge does seem to afford some protection to Job, but does this passage support the elaborate theology and practice of "praying a hedge" which is so common in many Christian circles?

What was this hedge and where did it come from? This hedge was clearly God's sovereign protection and blessing on Job. That is evident from the fact that Satan challenged God to remove such blessing and protection in order to show that Job would curse Him.

You can read the whole first chapter of Job and you will see that it is not a manual on spiritual warfare. The point of the passage is not to teach us how to pray effectively against Satan. In Job 1, we get a glimpse into the spiritual realm at something we cannot affect: God's sovereign protection of His people and the continuance or removal of that protection for His own sovereign and Self-glorifying purposes.

Job 1 does not prescribe spiritual warfare tactics. That is the furthest thing from the mind of the author and the context. Does the passage say that this hedge was made of thorns? No. Does the passage say that this hedge was placed in response to the spiritual warfare prayers of Job or of others on his behalf? No. In fact, this was the sovereign protection of God over Job, something Satan could not penetrate without God's permission. It was put in place by God and God alone and removed by God and God alone!

All that we can say about this hedge is that it refers to God's sovereign protection of Job and all that was his. We are not told to pray for this. Nor do we have any examples of someone praying for this. We simply see in this passage that Satan's reach is limited by the sovereign hand of God.

I argue that such a hedge is already the present possession of each individual believer - every saint. Satan would kill all of us if he could. What is it that prevents him from harming God's people or even killing them? Nothing but God's sovereign protection of His people. Why am I not dead right now? Why are my wife and kids preserved at any given moment? God keeps evil at bay by His sovereign hand. Satan is on a leash and it stretches no further than God allows. One lesson we learn from Job 1 is that if we are preserved from anything it is because God is protecting us. If we are not preserved from something, it is because God has allowed it.

Clearly it goes way beyond what is written to teach that such a protection against Satan can be constructed, and needs to be constructed through a specific mantra-style prayer in order to protect one from demonic influence and attack. Hosea 2 and Job 1 are not in any way connected. The hedge in one refers to protection, in the other, punishment. One refers to the sovereign protection of God upon possessions, the other refers to God moving to afflict people by removing their possessions. The only thing those two passages have in common is that neither of them teaches the practice of praying a hedge of thorns!

Biblical Interpretation Gone Awry

Notice how the practice of praying the hedge is "derived" from Scripture. The word "hedge" is mentioned in two totally unrelated passages. One of them also mentions thorns. Therefore, we must be able to pray a hedge of thorns around people to protect them. Huh?!

What if I told you that you needed to pray a tower next to someone to protect them from Satan. After all, Satan can't attack someone who has a tower prayed up next to them. How do I know? Because towers are for defense in the Bible. What verse teaches this? Well, the Bible describes towers that protect (Psalm 61:3) and the same psalm speaks of prayer (v. 1). Therefore we should pray towers over people for their protection so Satan can't successfully attack them.

If I started teaching that goofiness, you would rightly charge me with twisting Scripture and creating doctrines out of whole cloth. The mere mention of certain words in the Bible does not condone whatever practice we want to assign to those words. We must always ask, "What does that text teach?" Neither of the passages we have examined teach anything remotely connected to the modern practice of praying hedges around people.

A Prayer for Protection

So what about praying for protection? Does that mean it is unbiblical to pray for God to watch over us and protect us from the attacks of our spiritual enemies? Certainly not (Ezra 8:21-23). There is nothing wrong with praying for protection for one's self or others. The Psalms are filled with references to praying for protection from enemies.[5] These prayers have nothing to do with hedges and thorns, or even Satan and demons.

It is unbiblical to teach that "praying a hedge of thorns" around someone or something is necessary to advance the Kingdom of Christ or to halt the work of Satan. It is unbiblical to promote certain mantra prayers as an effective tool in the war against Satan. I take issue with the abuse of Hosea 2:6 and Job 1:10. That is a central issue.

Reforming Prayers

"Okay, so there might be no biblical justification for the practice, but does it really matter? Aren't we just splitting hairs? Certainly God knows what I mean and He can answer that prayer, right? What harm does it do to go on praying hedges of thorns around people?"

---

[5] Psalm 7, 17, 57, 59, 94, just to name a few. There are many.

It might not do any harm, but does it do any good? Why not pray a row of trees? Why not pray a field of grass - a big field that Satan will have to spend time traveling across before he gets to us? Why not pray a circle of tomato plants? Maybe Satan doesn't like tomato plants. Pardon my tongue-in-cheekness, but I am just trying to illustrate silliness by being silly.

Praying a hedge of thorns has no more biblical warrant than praying a circle of tomato plants. If there is no biblical warrant for it, why do it? Why teach others to do it, and why model it for others? We want our prayers to be guided by Scripture. We want to prosecute this battle according to the instructions of the Commander-in-Chief. We should concern ourselves with praying biblical prayers. The teaching of Scripture should guide our prayers. We ought to use the language of Scripture and pray for those things that are in keeping with the will of God as revealed in Scripture.

Now, I believe that it is God's will to protect His people. How does He do that? He does it through truth. When we embrace the truth, understand the truth, live the truth, and appropriate the truth, then we are taking every thought captive to obedience of Christ and waging effective warfare (2 Corinthians 10:3-5). We can pray for people the way that Paul did (Ephesians 1:15-23; 3:14-19; Philippians 1:3-11; Colossians 1:9-12). Remember, we are involved in a truth war - a battle for the minds of men waged with the truth, not imaginary hedges of thorns.

It is biblical to pray for God to sovereignly protect someone who is in danger. It is biblical to pray that God would deliver someone from the influence and power of Satan. It is biblical to pray that God would cause someone to come to a knowledge and love of the truth and to be delivered from lies. It is biblical to pray that men and women might hear the truth, understand the truth and be delivered from darkness to light, from the kingdom of Satan to the kingdom of Christ (Acts 26:18). Those are all biblical, intelligent, and meaningful prayers.

On the contrary, praying a "hedge of thorns" is neither meaningful nor biblical. It is stringing together a few words that happen to be mentioned in various Bible passages and using it as a prayer weapon. Satan does not fear such prayers!

Conclusion

Once again, if our Commander-in-Chief has not commissioned us to prosecute the war in this manner, what business do we have doing it? Do we know better than He? Dare we presume that our methods are superior to His? If this were an effective warfare tool, do you not think He would have told us about it? Would we have to wrench verses from their context and abuse their meaning in order to establish a practice commissioned by God? Never. The weapons of our warfare are not carnal.

6

Carnal Weapons: Hexes

The only exposure Ryan ever had to anything spiritual was rooted in the occult.[1] His mom and dad dabbled in occult practices such as tarot cards, ouija boards, and séances. His mother avidly read books on astrology, horoscopes, and New Age Spirituality.

Ryan's parents were by no means pioneers in the field from within their larger family. His maternal grandmother had boasted of being a wiccan high priestess, and though Ryan had never known his great-grandfather, he had heard about his involvement in these same practices from his father, who proudly followed in his grandfather's steps. All told, Ryan could count nearly a dozen family members who had some involvement in some form of spiritism, divination, astrology, or occultism.

Until he arrived at college and met his roommate, an evangelical Christian named Mark, Ryan had never met anyone who took the Bible seriously, let alone someone who diligently read it and attended Bible studies. Mark and Ryan began to have long discussions about spiritual realities, spirit beings, the occult and the Christian faith. After attending almost a dozen Bible studies with Mark, and a long lunchtime discussion with Mark's pastor, Ryan became convinced of his need for a Savior.

Ryan came to see the weight of his sin and his need for forgiveness and repented of his sin and embraced Jesus Christ as Savior and Lord. The radical difference in Ryan's conduct and outlook was immediately manifest. He had a hunger for the Bible like he had never had for anything in his life.

---

[1] Though the characters and circumstances of this story are fictional, they represent real events and real teachings that permeate the Christian Church.

As if a light had been turned on, Ryan suddenly saw the horrors of the spiritual entities that lay behind his parents' activities. He was grieved over the lost, deceived condition of not only his parents, but others in his family who were involved in the occult. Ryan's concern turned to fear, when, at his weekly Bible study, he heard a fellow student suggest that he may have inherited a demon from his parents. This Christian went on to explain that the punishment of God would be visited upon Ryan and his children because of his parents' sin of witchcraft, and unless Ryan specifically renounced the sins and demons of his parents, then Satan's influence would be allowed to continue for generations to come. To protect not only himself, but his future children, Ryan was encouraged to deal directly and specifically with demons that supposedly had become entrenched in his family by generations of occult practices.

Does any of this sound familiar? Have you been exposed to teaching like this on the subject of spiritual warfare?

Must I verbally renounce sins, demons, or curses in order to be delivered from them? Does God punish children (even those who have become believers) for the sins of their parents? Can a person inherit a demon? Does someone saved from an occult background need a further work of God in their lives to prevent satanic influence? What does the Bible mean when it says that God visits the sins of the parents on the children to the third and fourth generation (Exodus 20:5)?

I get asked these questions often by people who have been exposed at one point or another to this type of teaching. It is rather prolific in many Christian circles. Answering these questions deserves our focused attention.

The Teaching

Commonly referred to as "generational curses" or "generational sin," it is a part of a larger theology of spiritual warfare that includes binding Satan, performing exorcisms (even of Christians), and praying against territorial spirits.

The practice of renouncing generational sins or generational curses is based on Exodus 20:5. ". . . I the LORD your God, am a jealous God, visiting the iniquity of the fathers on the children, on the third and the fourth generations of those who hate me. "

Some use this verse to teach that God will punish children for the sins of their parents. Others go further, and teach that one can be under a curse because of their parents' sin: a curse which must be persistently renounced and fought against. Yet others go even further and teach that a child can actually inherit a demon from their parents, particularly if their parents were involved in sins of witchcraft or idolatry.

It is believed that unless the Christian consciously and verbally confesses in prayer the sins of their ancestors, and renounces those sins and all their attendant curses and consequences, Satan will have a "legal hold" in the believer's life which will keep that believer from spiritual freedom, sanctification, spiritual growth, and the blessings of God. This "legal hold" can result in demonic oppression and even demonic possession of a Christian.

Much is made of the dangers associated with adopting children, since demons can supposedly transfer through bloodlines and thus gain access to unsuspecting Christian homes.[2] After discussing the dangers of demons attaching themselves to adopted children, Mark Bubeck, in his book *The Adversary*, offers a recommended prayer of "Renunciation and Affirmation":

> As a child of God purchased by the blood of the Lord Jesus Christ, I here and now renounce and repudiate all the sins of my ancestors. As one who has been delivered from the power of darkness and translated into the kingdom of God's dear Son, I cancel out all demonic working that has been passed on to me from my ancestors. As one who has been crucified with Jesus Christ and raised to walk in newness of life, I cancel every curse that may have been put upon me. I announce to Satan and all his forces that Christ became a curse for me when He hung on the cross. As one who has been crucified and raised with Christ and now sits

---

[2] Mark I. Bubeck, *The Adversary* (Chicago: Moody Press, 1975), 147-148. Bubeck defines "transference" as "the passing on of demonic powers from one generation to the next" and then goes on to cite a number of anecdotes to prove his doctrine.

with Him in heavenly places, I renounce any and every way in which Satan may claim ownership of me. I declare myself to be eternally and completely signed over and committed to the Lord Jesus Christ. All this I do in the name and authority of the Lord Jesus Christ.[3]

Bubeck then includes this note: "None of us knows what works of Satan may have been passed on to him from his ancestry. Therefore, it is well for every child of God to make the above renunciation and affirmation. It is advisable to speak it out loud."[4]

Not one to shy away from offering special incantations for nearly any situation, a special and far more extensive prayer for adopted children or foster children is given along with this reminder: "A renunciation and affirmation of this type should often be a part of one's prayer ministry for his adopted child."[5]

This type of formulaic prayer is not unique to Mark Bubeck. It is also found prolifically in the writings of popular author Neil T. Anderson. In his book *Released From Bondage*, Anderson writes,

> The last step to freedom is to renounce the sins of your ancestors and any curses which may have been placed on you. . . . Familiar spirits can be passed on from one generation to the next if not renounced and your new spiritual heritage in Christ is not proclaimed. You are not guilty for the sin of any ancestor, but because of their sin, Satan has gained access to your family. . . . In addition, deceived people may try to curse you, or Satanic groups may try to target you.[6]

---

[3] Ibid., 148. This prayer was actually composed by Ernest B. Rockstad of Faith and Life Ministries in Andover, Kansas, whom Bubeck refers to as "one of God's most experienced veterans in this subject of warfare."

[4] Ibid., 149.

[5] Ibid., 150. Indeed, Anderson, Bubeck and White offer prayers for cleansing hotel rooms, houses, breaking curses, adopted children, foster children, bedtime, and a host of others. One quickly gets the impression that we would be lost without the formulaic incantations which are said to be of such great value against the demonic forces.

[6] Neil T. Anderson, *Released From Bondage* (Nashville: Thomas Nelson Publishers, 1993), 250-251.

Anderson even suggests formulaic prayers for cleansing apartments and houses that may have been formerly occupied by unbelievers and which might still carry a curse. Taking this unbiblical teaching to its logical conclusion, Anderson saddles the reader with this burden: "Adopted children can be especially subject to demonic strongholds because of their natural parentage. But even an adopted child can become a new creation in Christ, and must actively renounce old strongholds and embrace his or her inheritance as God's child."[7]

Like Bubeck, Anderson offers a prayer to effectively break the curse:

> I here and now reject and disown all the sins of my ancestors. As one who has been delivered from the power of darkness and translated into the kingdom of God's dear Son, I cancel out all demonic working that may have been passed on to me from my ancestors. . . . I renounce all satanic assignments that are directed toward me and my ministry, and I cancel every curse that Satan and his workers have put on me. I announce to Satan and all his forces that Christ became a curse for me. . . . I reject any and every way in which Satan may claim ownership of me. I belong to the Lord Jesus Christ, who purchased me with His own blood. I reject all of the blood sacrifices whereby Satan may claim ownership of me. I declare myself to be eternally and completely signed over and committed to the Lord Jesus Christ.[8]

In a section entitled "Generational Sin," Thomas B. White writes in his book *The Believer's Guide to Spiritual Warfare*,

> Those who have had experience with deliverance know that in some cases there are demonic powers that have worked within a family bloodline for many generations. This phenomenon is clinically documented. . . . If sin occurs, especially sin related to idolatry or witchcraft, and it

---

[7] Neil T. Anderson, *The Bondage Breaker* (Eugene, OR: Harvest House Publishers, 1990), 207.
[8] Ibid., 207-8.

remains unresolved, the enemy has a legal right to accuse and oppress. . . . We observe a connection between genealogical sin and oppression in current generations.[9]

I could multiply examples of this ad infinitum, ad nauseum! It is not difficult to see that there is "a new generation of Christians who are beginning to see the [spiritual] world through a grid that has more in common with Greek and Persian mystery religions than with Christianity."[10] Indeed! When did Christianity start resembling the dialog of a Harry Potter novel?

Exodus 20 in Context

As you read through the prayers above, you will notice language that comes directly out of Scripture: "I have been crucified with Christ," "translated into the kingdom of God's dear Son," etc. (Galatians 2:20; Colossians 1:13). Though the language might be gleaned from Scripture for some of the statements, that does not necessarily mean that the overall theology is biblical.

Does the Bible teach that demons and curses can be transferred though bloodlines? Can we inherit demons and curses? Must these curses be renounced verbally, forcefully, and repeatedly in order for the child of God to be free or protected from Satan?

The verse which serves as the linchpin in this theology, and one you will hear quoted constantly in support of this practice, is Exodus 20:5. I have found that the full context is seldom quoted and even less frequently understood. Here is the verse with its context:

> You shall not make for yourself an idol, or any likeness of what is in heaven above or on the earth beneath or in the water under the earth. You shall not worship them or serve them; for I, the Lord your God, am a jealous God, <u>visiting the iniquity of the fathers on the children, on the third and the fourth generations of those who hate Me</u>, but showing

---

[9] Thomas B. White, *The Believer's Guide to Spiritual Warfare* (Ann Arbor: Servant Publications, 1990), 62.

[10] Chuck Colson, J.I. Packer, R.C. Sproul, et. al., *Power Religion* (Chicago: Moody Press, 1992), 278.

lovingkindness to thousands, to those who love Me and keep My commandments (Exodus 20:4–6).

The underlined part of verse 5 is usually isolated from its context and used to teach that God visits punishments and curses on the descendants of those who hate Him, even to the fourth generation. Interestingly, and most telling, is the fact that verse 6 is almost entirely ignored by spiritual warfare teachers in explaining the meaning of verse 5. And verse 6 is not a separate paragraph, or even a separate sentence. It is the rest of the sentence of verse 5! A careful look at the passage will show that it has nothing at all to do with the modern teaching of "generational curses."

First, there is an obvious parallelism present between verse 5 and verse 6 that is central to understanding the meaning of the passage.

Verse 5 - "visit iniquity"
Verse 6 - "show lovingkindness"

Verse 5 - "to the fourth generation"
Verse 6 - "to the thousands"

Verse 5 - "of those who hate God"
Verse 6 - "of those who keep His Commandments"

This Hebrew parallelism contrasts two actions of God, two numbers of generations, and two groups of people. The two groups in contrast are "those who hate Me [God]" versus "those who keep My [His] commandments." The two numbers of generations contrasted are "the third and the fourth generations" versus "thousands." The two actions of God contrasted are "visit iniquity" versus "show lovingkindness."

There is nothing difficult to understand about this passage. It is a Jewish literary device used for expressing comparison and showing a preference for one thing over another. God would rather bless a thousand generations of those who love Him than curse three or four generations of those who hate Him. His preference is to bless those who keep His commandments.

Psalm 30:5 is another example of this comparative parallelism, "For His anger is but for a moment, His favor is for a lifetime; Weeping may last for the night, But a shout of joy comes in the morning." The abundance and enduring blessing of God's favor is highlighted when contrasted with God's anger.

Deuteronomy 7 expresses the same thing, though the order is reversed. Deuteronomy 7:9-10 says, "Know therefore that the Lord your God, He is God, the faithful God, who keeps His covenant and His lovingkindness to a thousandth generation with those who love Him and keep His commandments; but repays those who hate Him to their faces, to destroy them; He will not delay with him who hates Him, He will repay him to his face." This is the same thing expressed in Exodus 20, showing it is God's preference and nature to bless and show lovingkindness.

Second, it cannot be assumed that the ones punished in verse 5 are "righteous" people or believers. The most natural interpretation is that God would visit circumstantial punishments on those who hate Him.[11] We should not assume that those being punished are the righteous descendants of those who hated God. It would make more sense, and be in keeping with teaching from the rest of the Old Testament, that those being punished, even in the third and fourth generation, are also God-hating idolaters who have followed in the footsteps of their apostate parents.

Third, the interpretation of spiritual warfare teachers does not hold up when consistently applied. They will say that verse 5 teaches that a curse or demon can be transferred to children for three or four generations because of the sin or activities of ancestors. Yet they will not be consistent and take verse 6 in the same way! Would they also suggest that God will bless a thousand generations (in spite of their personal and persistent sin) because of the righteousness of one ancestor? Yet, to be consistent, they would have to affirm this. Verse

---

[11] Examples of these circumstantial punishments would include expulsion from the land and other punishments that would come from not keeping the Mosaic covenant (Deuteronomy 28:15-68).

6 says that God will show lovingkindness for a thousand generations because of the one who kept His commandments. If a Christian can be punished and afflicted because of the un-renounced sins of his father, grandfather, or great-grandfather, then will unbelieving descendants be blessed because of a righteous ancestor 597 generations ago? Certainly not!

Fourth, we notice the complete absence of any mention of demons or evil spirits, or even curses of the type Anderson and others suggest. The passage is not describing demonic strongholds, spiritual warfare, or how to renounce curses, but rather the Ten Commandments - not spirits, but sin and its consequent punishment. It is an unimaginable and unjustified stretch to take anything in this passage and build on it a theology regarding demons or generational curses.

Fifth, Scripture consistently teaches that each person is punished for his own sins, and not the sins of another. An essential passage on this very subject is Ezekiel 18. In Ezekiel's day people quoted a proverb: "The fathers eat sour grapes, but the children's teeth are set on edge" (18:2). They seemed to believe (wrongly) that though the fathers did the crime, the children were cursed or punished for it. Ezekiel spent 32 verses refuting this very teaching to show that "the soul that sins, it shall die" (18:4).

In contrast to modern "generational curse" teachers, Ezekiel affirms that, "The person who sins will die. The son will not bear the punishment for the father's iniquity, nor will the father bear the punishment for the son's iniquity; the righteousness of the righteous will be upon himself, and the wickedness of the wicked will be upon himself" (Ezekiel 18:20).

The Problems Are Many!

Anderson tries to show his practices are legitimate by citing similar examples from church history:

> The early church included in its public declaration of faith, "I renounce you, Satan, all your works and ways." The Catholic Church, the Eastern Orthodox Church, and many other liturgical churches still require this renunciation as

part of confirmation. For some reason it has disappeared from most evangelical churches. You must not only choose the truth but disavow Satan and his lies.[12]

I know why the practice vanished from Evangelicalism - because it is patently unbiblical!

Apart from the rampant quoting of Scripture out of context and abuse of those verses, there is a myriad of other problems with this theology. I'll begin with what I consider to be most offensive.

First, this theology denies the sufficiency of the cross, the atonement, and the gospel. This is the most serious and yet subtle error propagated by those who teach these doctrines. They would affirm vocally, and forcefully, that they do, in fact, believe in the power of the cross and the sufficiency of the gospel, but their practice is a patent denial of these very things.

Apparently one-time repentance from a life of sin, the cleansing of the blood of Christ, forgiveness of all sins - past, present, and future - is not sufficient in itself to free one from bondage to sin and the power of Satan. Something else is necessary, namely, reciting and renouncing verbally all the sins that the Holy Spirit will bring to one's mind. The prayers of renunciation must be spoken in order to break the power of Satan and eliminate his strongholds - to revoke his "legal right."

Scripture says that the one who trusts in Jesus Christ for salvation has been delivered from the kingdom of darkness and set free from him who had the power of death, namely the devil (Colossians 1:13; Hebrews 2:14-18). The child of God has been adopted into the family of God and is indwelt by the Spirit of the living God. The gospel has justified him freely, fully, and forever. To suggest that anything more is necessary apart from the gospel is an affront to the sufficiency of the work of Christ on the cross.

These renunciation and affirmation prayers allegedly accomplish things that Scripture says have already been accomplished and secured for the believer by the death of Christ. No further "work" on my behalf is necessary to effect that deliverance.

---

[12] *Released*, 70.

84

If the believer is in Christ, he is a new creation. All old things have passed away. Period. To suggest that without the verbal, specific renunciations of Satan, he will continue to have a "legal claim" on my family, possessions, and life is to say that the work of Christ did not break that "claim" (although, as we have seen, the whole idea of that "legal claim" is suspect from the beginning)!

What is the significance of being in Christ, if freedom from Satan is not secured in Him? What good does the work of Christ actually do if I need to further continually renounce sins and curses and cleanse my surroundings of Satan's strongholds through incantation-like prayers?

Second, this theology is an attack on the sufficiency of Scripture. You will search the Bible in vain for any of the prayers offered by Anderson, Bubeck, and others. There are no prayers for renouncing curses, protecting adopted children, cleansing houses, apartments, or hotel rooms, or binding Satan from dreams. There are no prayers offered for canceling Satan's claims, demonic curses, or generational-bloodline-demonic influences. Not one. Not only do we not find any examples of them, we are never told to pray such prayers.

As Ice and Dean point out, "In fact, there is not one example in the entire Bible of a saved person being under a satanic curse which had to be broken by Christian exorcism or distinct confession.[13]

One is left to wonder how ill equipped we would be without all the incantations, prayers, and formulas offered by spiritual warfare teachers. We are told they are essential, and yet we don't find them in Scripture - only in the books by "spiritual warfare experts." Without those books, countless millions would live lives of bondage to Satan and his generational demons and curses, and that because all they had was the Bible! Imagine!

Anderson makes the following claim: "To be completely free from the past, we have found it *necessary* for each person to specifically renounce every false religion, false teacher, false practice and every means of false guidance that he or she has participated

---

[13] Thomas Ice and Robert Dean, *Overrun By Demons: The Church's New Preoccupation With The Demonic* (Eugene: Harvest House Publishers, 1990), 181.

in." [14] In my opinion, this reveals incredible hubris. It may be unintended, but it is hubris nonetheless. When someone teaches that something outside of Scripture - not commanded, illustrated or patterned in Scripture - is necessary for our sanctification and deliverance, he is saying that Scripture is not sufficient. He is implicitly claiming that God neglected to provide us with information necessary for our life in Christ. But do not fret! We have Anderson to thank for providing what the Holy Spirit overlooked.

Third, this theology leads to bondage, not freedom. Though these spiritual warfare teachers would say that this teaching helps to set people free, "it instead binds them to a superstitious worldview where Satan is not only present on every front, but he must repeatedly be renounced on each and every one of those fronts or he will control them."[15]

Christians are unwittingly adopting a pagan, mystical, voodoo-magic-type worldview in the area of spiritual warfare. They are being encouraged to constantly fear the power, curses, influence, presence, and claims of Satan over them, their possessions, and their family. Without the uttering of incantations, formulaic prayers, and constant renunciations, they can never hope to be free, resulting in bondage to a patently unbiblical worldview and theology of angels and demons.

Fourth, this is an insult to adopted children everywhere! To burden adoptive parents with the unbiblical and unjustified fear that their adopted child could be carrying some "bloodline curse" which requires special attention not procured at the cross is cruel at best.

The theology of generational curses, generational sins, renunciation prayers, hexes, and curses is completely unbiblical. The cross has secured your salvation, justification, deliverance, sanctification, glorification, and total freedom from the kingdom of darkness. Those in Christ are delivered. Period. Having professed

---

[14] Neil T. Anderson, *Helping Others Find Freedom in Christ* (Ventura, CA: Regal Books, 1995), 247. Emphasis added.

[15] Elliot Miller, "Spiritual Warfare and the Seven Steps To Freedom," *Christian Research Journal* 21.3 (1999), 16.

and embraced Christ, you need not renounce anything. You are new and complete in Him. Rest in it - without fear!

7

Carnal Weapons: Binding Satan

No analysis of modern spiritual warfare methodology would be complete without a look at the practice of "binding Satan." To say that this practice enjoys popularity in charismatic circles is to state the obvious, but of all the false practices of modern spiritual warfare teachers, this one enjoys immense popularity in both charismatic and non-charismatic circles.

As with the other practices we have examined, we want to allow Scripture to be our guide as we seek to bring our beliefs and practices under the authority of God's truth. When we do this, we find there is no biblical teaching and no example in Scripture for binding Satan.

What Is this "Binding" Thing?

I have no doubt that most Christians today are familiar with the practice of binding Satan. You have probably heard this during a prayer meeting, Bible study, devotional time, and even from a pulpit during a Sunday service. "The practice of binding Satan and/or the demons and evil spirits is not only something which Christians do during public and private deliverance sessions, but it is often a personal activity exercised on a regular basis by a growing number of Christians."[1]

It is believed that by binding Satan, his activity is limited, hindered, or prohibited in the sphere in which he is bound. For instance, a person might pray that Satan will be bound from blinding a person to whom they wish to present the gospel with the belief that this will improve the likelihood that the person will trust Christ as

---

[1] Thomas Ice and Robert Dean, *Overrun By Demons: The Church's New Preoccupation With The Demonic* (Eugene: Harvest House Publishers, 1990), 100.

Savior. Someone might pray that Satan would be bound from a certain event (concert, worship service, etc.) and thus prohibited from having any influence or power over that event. Or someone might pray that Satan be bound from a geographical location (a new house, a neighborhood, a church, bedroom, workplace, or hotel room) with the belief that uttering such a prayer cripples Satan's ability to interfere or enter.[2]

The prayer might be anything from an innocent desire expressed to God, to a direct command to Satan. I have heard people pray both ways. I used to know a man who, innocently enough, would humbly ask God, "Lord, would you bind Satan from having any influence here?" On the other end of the spectrum are the nearly insane rantings of televangelist Robert Tilton directed toward the demonic forces that he believes are attacking his followers in TV-land:

> Satan, you demonic spirits of AIDS[3], and AIDS virus - I bind you! You demon-spirits of cancer, arthritis, infection, migraine headaches, pain - come out of that body! Come out of that child! Come out of that man. . . Satan, I bind you! You foul demon-spirits of sickness and disease, infirmities in the inner ear and the lungs and the back. You demon-spirits of arthritis, sickness, and disease. You tormenting infirm spirits in the stomach. Satan, I bind you! You nicotine spirits - I bind you! In the name of Jesus![4]

Even the very conservative teacher, Bill Gothard, advocates the practice of binding Satan by the name and blood of Jesus Christ. In his book *Rebuilders Guide*, Gothard offers "The Prayer to Bind Satan and Build a 'Hedge of Thorns,'": "Heavenly Father, I ask You to

---

[2] Ibid. If this is starting to sound eerily similar to the spiritual worldview of those who advocate renouncing generational curses, you are on to something. A similar view of the demonic rests at the foundation of both these practices.

[3] The Bible does not teach that all illnesses and infirmities are the result of demonic oppression or possession.

[4] Robert Tilton, *Success-N-Life Program* (ca. 1991), video on file at the Christian Research Institute. Hank Hanegraaff, *Christianity In Crisis* (Eugene: Harvest House Publishers, 1993), 257.

rebuke and bind Satan in the name and through the blood of the Lord Jesus Christ."[5]

Gothard cites Mark 3:27 and Jude 9 in support of the practice[6] and writes, "Before we attempt to reclaim a loved one who has come under Satan's power, we must first bind Satan. Otherwise, he works through that loved one to create a reaction toward every attempt of restoration." What will happen if you don't bind Satan before trying to restore a loved one? Gothard answers, "Attempting to spoil Satan's house without binding him will only result in arguments."[7]

My intention is not to pick on Bill Gothard. Frankly, I could quote a number of rather conservative teachers who would parrot that advice. The teaching has crept into every nook and cranny of the Church.

Spiritual warfare teacher Mark I. Bubeck,[8] while telling a story about a suicidal "Christian" who called him in the middle of the night for advice, records the following about that conversation: "I prayed with him, binding up all of Satan's powers that were seeking to destroy him."[9] In the same book, while giving a list of "dos and don'ts" for dealing with the demonic in confrontation warfare, Bubeck instructs us, "Do bind all powers of darkness working under any wicked spirit to him, commanding them all to leave when he does."[10]

Like Bubeck, Neil T. Anderson's entire approach to spiritual warfare is based on the presumed authority of the believer over the devil. Anderson teaches, "God has granted us the authority to 'bind

---

[5] Bill Gothard, *Rebuilder's Guide* (United States: Institute in Basic Life Principles, Inc., 2005), 119. He further suggests that you pray, "I ask You to build a 'hedge of thorns' around my partner, so that anyone with wrong influence will lose interest in him (or her) and leave." Like others, Gothard distorts and misuses Hosea 2:5-7 to promote the practice of hedge-praying. See Chapter 6.

[6] These verses, as we will see, offer no justification at all for this practice. The subject of rebuking Satan will be handled in Chapter 8.

[7] Ibid., 154. Gothard then quotes Matthew 7:3-5, Mark 3:27 and Ephesians 6:12 in support of this claim. What do those verses have to do with this assertion? Your guess is as good as mine.

[8] He was featured heavily in Chapter 6 for his absurd teaching on generational curses.

[9] Mark I. Bubeck, *The Adversary* (Chicago: Moody Press, 1975), 91. Emphasis mine.

[10] Ibid., 125.

what shall be bound in heaven' . . . The effectiveness of binding the strongman (see Matthew 12:20 [sic]) is dependent upon the leading of the Holy Spirit and subject to the scope and limits of the written Word of God."[11]

True to his style, Anderson offers a formulaic prayer which supposedly binds Satan from interfering with loved ones:

> We agree that every evil spirit that is in or around (name) be bound to silence. They cannot inflict any pain, speak to (name)'s mind, or prevent (name) from hearing, seeing or speaking. Now in the name of the Lord Jesus Christ I command you, Satan, and all your hosts to release (name) and remain bound and gagged so that (name) will be able to obey God.[12]

If you ever tune in to CBN (Christian Broadcasting Network) in hopes of being exposed to sound theology, you'll be sorely disappointed. During one broadcast of *The 700 Club*, Pat Robertson advocated binding Satan in order to deal with a satanic attack within one's home. During the "Bring It On" segment, Robertson was asked this question by "Gilbert": "Our household has been under attack lately by the devil. Are we supposed to rebuke the devil in Jesus' name or just look to God to take care of the matter for us?"[13]

Robertson responded by saying,

> I think you need to wage spiritual warfare and you need to understand what you are doing. But, uh, I,. . . I ,. . . I, think we should say, if you want something to say, is, 'I bind you, Satan and the forces of evil, and, uh, In the name of Jesus, I bind your power', which means you nullify the power of

---

[11] Elliot Miller, "Spiritual Warfare and the Truth Encounter," *Christian Research Journal* 21.2 (1999), 13. Taken from "Twenty Five Most Popular Questions," Freedom in Christ website, http://www.ficm.org. I searched and could not find this on Anderson's website any longer.

[12] Neil T. Anderson, *The Bondage Breaker* (Eugene, OR: Harvest House Publishers, 1990), 227, as quoted in Elliot Miller, "Spiritual Warfare and the Truth Encounter," *Christian Research Journal* 21.2 (1999), 14-15.

[13] http://www.cbn.com/media/player/index.aspx?s=/vod/BIO_010510_WS

what he's exercising against you. . . . That is the way you deal with this situation.[14]

Proof Texts to the Rescue!

Those who teach and practice this method of dealing with the devil will typically offer a few standard Bible verses as biblical support. Here they are:

Matthew 12:29: "Or how can anyone enter the strong man's house and carry off his property, unless he first binds the strong man? And then he will plunder his house."[15]

Matthew 16:19: "I will give you the keys of the kingdom of heaven; and whatever you bind on earth shall have been bound in heaven, and whatever you loose on earth shall have been loosed in heaven."

Matthew 18:18: "Truly I say to you, whatever you bind on earth shall have been bound in heaven; and whatever you loose on earth shall have been loosed in heaven."

You will notice immediately the mention of "strong man," "bind," "binding in Heaven," and "binding on earth." These phrases are all that is needed by some to build an entire theology of spiritual warfare that involves formulaic prayers to bind Satan. However, a proper interpretation of each passage in its context yields an entirely different understanding of Jesus' words. We'll take a look at each one.

Matthew 12:29 and Context[16]

Matthew 12:29: "Or how can anyone enter the strong man's house and carry off his property, unless he first binds the strong man? And then he will plunder his house."

As the teaching goes, Satan is the strong man, and sinners are his possession. In order to rescue loved ones from his grasp and influence, we must first "bind Satan" so that he cannot resist our

---

[14] Ibid.

[15] Mark 3:27 cited by Gothard is parallel to Matthew 12:29.

[16] For the sake of space, I will not quote the entire context which properly includes 12:22-42. However, I would strongly encourage you to read the verses yourself and follow along in the text as I explain the passage.

effort to "plunder his house." When verse 29 is all that is read, then it is easy to see how people could be led to the false conclusion that this passage is describing the modern practice of binding Satan. In reality, nothing of the sort is being described.

The context of Matthew 12 has nothing to do with spiritual warfare at all. This is a record of an historical event in the life of the Lord Jesus in which He healed a demon-possessed man. The crowd began to wonder if Jesus was who He claimed to be: the Son of David (12:23). That was the proper conclusion, but not the one that the Pharisees wanted the people to reach. In an attempt to dissuade the crowd from concluding that Jesus was the Messiah, they offered an alternate explanation of His ability to cast out demons saying, "This man casts out demons only by Beelzebul the ruler of demons" (12:24).

To show the lunacy of such a charge, Jesus pointed out that everything He did as a demonstration of His Messianic credentials was directly opposed to Satan. Why would Satan cast out Satan (12:26)? Why would he fight against himself by empowering Christ to wage war against Satan since, clearly, everything that Christ did, opposed Satan's works and power? How could such a kingdom stand (12:25)?

Surely Jesus must be stronger than Satan if He was able to come into this world and war so effectively against his kingdom and plunder his captives. Jesus was not *empowered* by Satan, but was *overpowering* Satan. That is the meaning of verse 29. True, Satan is the strong man in the verse, but the binding is an analogy to show Christ's strength over Satan, not a command or example that we are to follow! Jesus was not instructing us about how to handle Satan. He was refuting the claim that His power came from the devil!

The central issue of the passage is, "By whose power did Christ perform His miracles - God's or Satan's?" Jesus offered a simply analogy. It must be by God's power, since only God is strong enough to destroy and plunder Satan's kingdom. The pharisees charged Jesus with *building* Satan's kingdom. Jesus claimed that He was ransacking Satan's kingdom.

Matthew 12:29 is not a universal command to all believers on how to effectively deal with the "strongman," but an historic illustration of Christ's personal power over Satan. Any use of that verse to support the practice of binding Satan is at best doing violence to the context!

Matthew 16:19 and Context[17]

Matthew 16:19: "I will give you the keys of the kingdom of heaven; and whatever you bind on earth shall have been bound in heaven, and whatever you loose on earth shall have been loosed in heaven."

Advocates of binding methodology wrongly say that Jesus is giving instructions on how to "build His church" (v. 18) which can only happen if we bind Satan on earth so that he will be bound in Heaven (heavenlies). This is taken as a mandate for believers to bind Satan with the accompanying promise that when we do, he will be bound by Heaven.

A quick look at the context reveals that these words were uttered in response to Peter's great confession that Jesus is "the Christ, the Son of the Living God" (16:16). It is in response to Peter's confession of Christ that Jesus utters the words in verse 19. Since Jesus is responding to Peter's confession, whatever the "binding" and "loosing" refers to, it must have to do with Jesus building his church (v. 18).

We notice again the context has nothing whatsoever to do with spiritual warfare. Jesus was not giving His disciples instruction on how to conquer Satan. That notion is completely foreign to the text. Spiritual warfare is not mentioned, nor even alluded to. Not to be deterred by the context, modern spiritual warfare experts ignore the subject at hand and read into the text a mandate for "binding warfare."

The key to the passage is in the terms "bind" (δεο, Gk.) and "loose" (λυο, Gk.) As Ice and Dean note, "That was a phrase used in Christ's day by Israel's religious leaders regarding what was

---

[17] For the sake of space, I will not quote the entire context which properly includes 16:13-20. However, I would strongly encourage you to read the verses yourself and follow along in the text as I explain the passage.

forbidden (bound) and what was permitted (loosed)."[18] These words need to be understood in the first century Jewish context in which they were spoken. This meant something to Peter and the original readers that had nothing to do with hindering or limiting Satan's activity through a magical formula uttered in prayer.

In connection with the use of these words in Matthew 16:19 and 18:18, the *Theological Dictionary of the New Testament* says, "Jesus does not give to Peter and the other disciples any power to enchant or to free by magic. The customary meaning of the Rabbinic expressions is equally incontestable, namely, to declare forbidden or permitted, and thus to impose or remove an obligation, by a doctrinal decision."[19] Peter, as a representative of the Apostles, was given a certain degree of authority, to make doctrinal declarations and obligations in the church.[20]

New Testament Greek scholar Dr. A.T. Robertson explains the significance of the tense of the verbs that are used: "Note the future perfect indicative (ἔσται δεδεμενον, ἔσται λελυμενον [estai dedemenon, estai lelumenon]), a state of completion. All this assumes, of course, that Peter's use of the keys will be in accord with the teaching and mind of Christ."[21]

A literal, but awkward, translation into English would read, ". . . whatever you bind on earth is that which shall already have been bound in the heavens, and whatever you loose on earth is that which shall already have been loosed in the heavens."[22] Peter was to forbid on earth, in the church, only that which Heaven had forbidden. He was to allow on earth, in the church, only that which Heaven had allowed.[23]

---

[18] Ice and Dean, 101.

[19] G. Kittel, G. W. Bromiley & G. Friedrich, Ed., *Vol. 2: Theological Dictionary of the New Testament* (Grand Rapids, MI: Eerdmans, 1964-) (electronic ed.), 60.

[20] We see this in practice in Acts 15 at the Jerusalem Council where the issue of Gentile salvation and circumcision were determined by the Apostles as they did declare the mind of God on a doctrinal issue and thus permitted certain things and forbid others.

[21] A. Robertson, *Word Pictures in the New Testament* (Matthew 16:19)(Oak Harbor: Logos Research Systems, 1997).

[22] Ice and Dean, 102.

[23] This, in no way, supports the notion that Peter was to function as the first Pope with the type of papal authority assumed by the Roman Catholic Church. This very same authority is

This is how the phrase was used in the first century Jewish community. This is how Jesus used the phrase. It has nothing at all to do with spiritual warfare or anything we do to Satan. It was a rabbinic phrase that had to do with being given the authority and responsibility to declare on earth those things that Heaven determined to be allowed (loosed) and forbidden (bound). To use this passage to teach a spiritual warfare methodology whereby Satan's activity is curtailed by our "binding prayer" is to misuse the passage.

Matthew 18:18 and Context[24]

Matthew 18:18, "Truly I say to you, whatever you bind on earth shall have been bound in heaven; and whatever you loose on earth shall have been loosed in heaven."

"Binding" and "loosing" are used in exactly the same way in this passage as they are in Matthew 16:19. It is the same idea, but here the practical application is to the practice of church discipline.

Jesus is saying that believers can have confidence that when they justly excommunicate someone on earth, they are fulfilling the will of God which has already been determined in Heaven. This should give them confidence in what they are doing. So in this context binding and loosing carry the idea which corresponds to our modern judicial language of declaring someone guilty (binding) or innocent (loosing). . . . In both passages neither word is referring to the contemporary idea of binding Satan or the demonic. Instead, these references refer to carrying out God's heavenly will upon earth as it has already been determined in Heaven.[25]

---

given in the context of the individual local church in its practice of church discipline in the next passage we will look at - Matt. 18:18. Every believer is to declare on earth what has been determined in Heaven. We know what these things are because the will of God has been revealed to us in Scripture through the Apostles.

[24] For the sake of space, I will not quote the entire context which properly includes 16:15-20. However, I would strongly encourage you to read the verses yourself and follow along in the text as I explain the passage.

[25] Ice and Dean, 102.

Like the others, this passage has nothing to do with spiritual warfare and binding Satan. Such flagrant abuse of Scripture ought to deeply concern the child of God!

The Problems are Legion

There are a number of practical and common-sense problems with this practice of binding Satan.

First, spiritual warfare teachers who advocate binding Satan based upon these passages utter nary a word about the "loosing" part of the verses. Yet the same passages that supposedly give authority to bind Satan mention loosing as well. In their theology, to what could this possibly refer? Does it refer to having the authority to loose Satan? What fool, having bound him, would then, in prayer, turn him loose? I have heard many Christians pray for Satan's binding, but I have never heard one pray, "I loose thee, Satan, in the name and blood of Jesus Christ, so you can return to your normal activities of deception and destruction." Yet if the passages cited give authority to bind the devil, what is the loosing in these passages intended to do?

Second, there is no single example anywhere in the Bible where an apostle or a prophet bound Satan. We never hear Jesus utter these words. We have a number of prayers recorded in the New Testament and not once do we read of them "binding Satan." Certainly if this practice were necessary for the advancement of the gospel and the success of the preaching enterprise, it would have been done before Paul's missionary journeys. If this were an essential methodology, we would expect to find the church employing it in response to persecution or prior to gatherings for worship. Yet we read nothing of it in the book of Acts. Nothing.

Simply put, we have no commands to do it, no teaching regulating it, and no examples of it. There are no chains, ropes, cables, or handcuffs in the armor of God (Ephesians 6:10-17).

Third, Scripture describes Satan as "roaming about," not bound by believers. Peter warns Christians in 1 Peter 5:8 to "be of sober spirit, be on the alert. Your adversary, the devil, prowls around like a roaring lion, seeking someone to devour." If Satan can be bound by merely uttering the phrase, "I bind Satan," then this warning is meaningless. Indeed, with all the binding going on today in Christian circles, one has to wonder in what sense he is prowling around seeking someone to devour.

Fourth, the only time that Scripture says that Satan is bound is during the 1,000-year millennial reign of Christ after this present age.[26] That binding is not said to be the work of believers, but of an angel on behalf of Jesus. He is bound for a specific period of time (1,000 years) which ends his present deceptive activity entirely (v. 3). This event is not something presently taking place, but something yet future. During the present age, Satan roams to and fro throughout the earth, deceiving and engaging in all his activities (Job 1:7).

Fifth, this practice doesn't even pass the "common sense test." For instance, how long does this binding last? Apparently, the binding is not permanent, since it needs to be done before every service, special event, or witness encounter. It must not be universal either, since binding Satan from one person does not seem to prohibit him from attacking or influencing someone else.

For as much as Satan is bound, he seems to be awfully productive and active. Is someone loosing him? Are demons setting him free? If so, we should just bind all demons and Satan, from everything, everyone, everywhere, and every event. There, problem solved! Does anyone really think this will work? This whole practice begins to look silly and useless quickly.

To even begin to answer any of these questions, and explain how and why and where this works, requires that people go *outside* Scripture and invent answers from their own imagination. None of the above questions can be answered from the Bible!

It Is Not Harmless but Dangerous

At this point someone might object by suggesting that the whole practice seems very harmless. After all, what does it really matter if someone does this?

---

[26] Revelation 20:1-10.

I contend that nothing is actually going on when people pray or command that Satan be bound. The real question is not, "What harm does it do?" but, "What good does it do?"

There is nothing in Scripture that suggests these binding prayers do anything at all. If it is a completely ineffective, meaningless mess of hocus-pocus (as I contend that it is), why would you do it? It is useless. Nothing happens! The Bible does not teach or model the use of this technique at all. It is an unproven (and dangerous) assumption that extra-biblical practices can be used to wage effective spiritual warfare. We are told to do God's will God's way, not to invent our own means out of whole cloth.

2 Corinthians 10:3-5 tells us how spiritual warfare is to be waged. It is a truth war. Disobeying God's instruction and adopting man-made means is not waging the war in the manner given by our Commander-in-Chief. It is disobedience.

This practice is not taught in Scripture, and we have no reason to believe it actually accomplishes anything at all. Advocates of "binding" methodology must answer this question: "Do I practice this because these passages, taken in their contexts, clearly teach this practice, or do I practice this because I want to believe it actually does something?" I suspect it is the latter, for it is certainly not taught in Scripture.

8

Carnal Weapons: Rebuking Satan

Kim Riddlebarger says there is "a new generation of Christians who are beginning to see the world [spiritual] through a grid that has more in common with Greek and Persian mystery religions than with Christianity."[1] It is almost as if mysticism has been wedded with Christianity, resulting in some hybrid we might call Mystianity. In no area is this more evident than in the realm of modern spiritual warfare methodologies. The approach to spiritual warfare so uncritically embraced by the bulk of modern evangelicalism has more in common with pagan mysticism than anything remotely biblical.

By this point, you have probably noticed that the approach I am advocating toward spiritual warfare is worlds apart from that which is practiced in most churches, taught by most pastors, and embraced by most spiritual warfare "experts." I believe that spiritual warfare is primarily a truth war that we wage against false ideologies by the proclamation of divine truth (2 Corinthians 10:3-5). People are delivered, once and for all, from darkness to light through the gospel, not through repetitive reciting of incantation-like prayers, renunciations, and mantras - however laden such phrases might be with Christian verbiage.

Sadly, the average Christian view of spiritual warfare involves hand-to-hand combat with demons as we storm the gates of hell, battle devils, and directly engage Satan and his hoard. This is done by verbally renouncing sins, curses, and demonic strongholds. Believers are told to pray a hedge of thorns, bind Satan through

---

[1] Chuck Colson, J.I. Packer, R.C. Sproul, et. al., *Power Religion* (Chicago: Moody Press, 1992), 278.

specific "binding prayers," and rebuke him. Christians are taught to pray against territorial spirits, name demons, and, of course, the perennial favorite, exorcise demons.[2] We have already analyzed the practices of praying hedges, renouncing curses, and binding Satan. Now we turn our attention to the practice of "rebuking Satan."

What Is "Rebuking Satan?"

It is believed by many modern spiritual warfare teachers that the believer's authority in Christ provides us with power over Satan and demons. This power can be used to force demonic powers to obey our commands, just as they obeyed those of Jesus and the apostles. The emphasis that many place on "binding Satan" is one manifestation of this view of the believer's authority. Supposedly we can limit and stop Satan's activities with simple commands such as, "I bind you, Satan, by the blood and name of Jesus Christ." It is also assumed that this authority gives believers the power to command and control demons during battle, to verbally rebuke the devil, to exorcise demons, and even to command the obedience of irrational and inanimate objects.

Spiritual warfare "expert", Neil T. Anderson, advocates prayers that involve directly speaking to Satan out loud. In his book, *The Bondage Breaker*, Anderson argues that

> The Word of God is the only offensive weapon mentioned in the list of armor. Since Paul used "rhema" instead of "logos" for "word" in Ephesians 6:17, I believe Paul is referring to the spoken Word of God instead of the Word of God personified in Jesus. We are to defend ourselves against the evil one by speaking aloud God's truth . . . You can communicate with God in your mind and spirit because He knows the thoughts and intents of your heart (Hebrews 4:12). Your unspoken communion with God is your private sanctuary; Satan cannot eavesdrop on you. But by the same token, if you only tell Satan to leave with

---

[2] It is difficult not to notice how much emphasis falls on Satan and his demons with this approach. He very quickly becomes the focus of a believer's mind when so much effort is directed toward dealing with him.

your thoughts, he won't leave because he can't hear you. You must defeat Satan by speaking out. The good news is that most attacks occur at night or when you are alone [this is good news?], so resisting Satan aloud seldom results in your having to explain to other people a vocal command instructing Satan to leave. However, there may be times when you will need to take a public stand against the enemy, which may include confessing with your mouth that Jesus is Lord (Romans 10:9).[3]

Anderson's treatment of Scripture in this section is lamentable. The Word of God in Ephesians 6 is the Word which God has spoken and not the words that a believer speaks, and therefore has nothing to do with believers mentally or vocally repeating those words.

False teachers among the Word Faith Movement are well known for rebuking Satan and his demons and presuming their authority in Christ to command demons to heed their will. Benny Hinn, at his Holy Spirit Miracle Cure in Rome, Italy, said while supposedly healing a woman of cancer, "We rebuke this spirit of cancer in the name of Jesus Christ the Son of God. . . I command it to go out of her."[4]

A search online for "rebuking Satan" will reveal a host of deliverance-ministry teaching on the subject. For instance, Britt Merrick writes on his May 19, 2010 blog,

When we are called upon to deal with demons while we are on mission for Christ, we should deal with them the same way that Christ did. Jesus *verbally commanded* demons to leave (Mark 5:8). Subsequently, we see the church in Acts following this same model (Acts 16:16-18). The model that we have set before us is the *verbal command* and rebuke of demons.[5]

---

[3] Neil T. Anderson, *The Bondage Breaker* (Eugene, OR: Harvest House Publishers, 1990), 84-85.

[4] Video available online at http://www.youtube.com/watch?v=Uw-B7sEAZO0.

[5] http://brittmerrick.com/brittmerrick/?p=872. Emphasis mine.

In attempting to answer the question, "Why does God ask us to speak directly to demons?" Merrick says,

There is nothing in Scripture that indicates that demons can hear our thoughts, read our minds, or be conscious of our inner dialogue. We must *rebuke them by speaking out loud*. Jesus gave us authority to cast out demons in His name (Mark 16:17) and displayed for us the model of *verbally commanding* them.[6]

This is representative of the theology of various deliverance ministries. The practice is widely accepted within charismatic circles.

I was surprised to find this theology applied in a very unique manner in a special issue of *The Voice of the Martyrs*. Richard Wurmbrand, founder of The Voice of the Martyrs, wrote an article entitled "Rebuking the Devil."[7] Wurmbrand believed that Christians have authority to command, bind, and rebuke devils. Beyond that, he attempted to prove that when we speak the Word of God in the name of Jesus, whatever we speak to must obey our command, even if it is an inanimate object! He told a story to support his claim.

American pastor Dick Eastman was much burdened about a thick wall that divided the capital of a civilized nation - the Berlin Wall erected by the Communists. Knowing that it separated families and friends, he pleaded with God: "It is written that if we pray You should move a mountain, it will move. So many pray for this. Why don't You fulfill Your promise?"

One night Jesus replied, "I never promised that I would move mountains if you pray. I said, 'If you (not Me) say to

---

[6] Ibid. Emphasis mine.

[7] All the following quotes from Richard Wurmbrand are taken from *The Voice of the Martyrs*, Special Issue, 1994. I have a tremendous amount of respect and admiration for Richard Wurmbrand and all that he has done to assist the persecuted church around the world and inform believers in free countries of the plight of our persecuted brethren. I have no doubt that Mr. Wurmbrand was a godly man who feared the Lord and served Him faithfully. I do, however, take issue with his approach to spiritual warfare, the practices he advocated, and his sad mishandling of Scripture in this particular issue of his publication.

this mountain, "Move!" It will move' (Matthew 17:20). Don't come to Me. Speak to the Berlin Wall."[8]

Pastor Eastman went all the way to Berlin to convince the wall to crumble. It did not. He complained to Jesus, who replied, "I did not say that you alone should do it. Take a few believers with you."[9]

The pastor went to Berlin a second time in the company of a few more believers and commanded the Berlin Wall to crumble. The group made a sign of the cross on the stone before which they had spoken.

After a few days the wall was no more. Germany was reunited.

Many factors contributed to the destruction of the infamous wall, but who can deny that a word spoken to an inanimate object may play a decisive role?

Actually, with all due respect, I would deny that! I don't believe for a moment that we have the power to affect inanimate objects by speaking God's Word to them. Taking Jesus' words about moving mountains in such a wooden, literal sense is to abuse His Word! Later in that same article, Wurmbrand wrote, "We too can speak to inanimate objects, even at great distances." One wonders then why Pastor Eastman had to fly to Germany - twice!

---

[8] Notice that Eastman is claiming Jesus spoke divine revelation to him concerning the meaning of a text in Scripture. Such direct revelation puts Eastman's claims above Scripture and beyond critique. After all, who are we to question what Jesus Himself spoke to Dick Eastman?

During my third year of Bible college, our class attended a large missions conference in Calgary, Alberta, at which Dick Eastman was the much-hyped keynote speaker. During one of the plenary sessions, I heard Eastman tell this very same story and make these same extraordinary claims, including that he was the instrument that God used to bring down the Berlin Wall!

[9] Oh, if Jesus had only been more clear the first time that He spoke to Eastman! He could have saved some money on airfare! Why didn't Jesus make His will clear? Did Jesus forget to tell Eastman to take others? Of course, common sense dives out the window when you accept by default that someone is receiving personal revelation from God.

What possible biblical warrant could Wurmbrand offer for these teachings? He writes,

Jesus commanded a tree to wither and it did. He commanded a storm to stop and there was peace.

But He did more than that. At one point He had a conversation with the devil. What we have in Matthew 4 might be only a resume⏤when in essence Jesus quoted the Word to him, and he was forced to retreat. On another occasion He rebuked a devil who inhabited a child and the devil left him immediately (Matthew 17:18).

Devils are intelligent beings. They understand what we say. *We too can make them obey our commands. . . .* If Jesus is living in us by His Spirit, *we too can command devils to depart.*[10]

The assumption behind all of the above teaching is that if Jesus did something while here on earth, we too, have authority to do the same. If Jesus spoke to a storm and calmed the sea, then we can speak to objects and command their obedience to our wills.[11] I wonder, then, why Mr. Wumbrand and Dick Eastman do not multiply bread and fish to feed the hungry multitudes all over the world. Why wouldn't either of them travel to the persecuted church and speak the Word of God to prison doors and prison guards, and free Christians held in chains? Why didn't Mr. Wumbrand simply command his own prison doors to open while he was held captive? That would be the logical conclusion we would draw from his theology.

Jesus performed signs which were intended to attest to His messianic claims. Such signs were the prerogative of the incarnate Son of God and never intended to be the norm for believers of every age. It is a sad abuse of the biblical texts to suggest that these things are examples for believers to follow today.[12]

---

[10] Emphasis mine.

[11] This is eerily similar to the theology of the Word Faith Movement that causes teachers like Kenneth and Gloria Copeland to claim the ability to command weather and storms to obey them.

[12] The same assumption lies behind the belief that we should be conducting exorcisms. If Jesus and the Apostles exorcised demons, then we also should be actively engaged in bold

Spiritual warfare expert Mark Bubeck shares a personal story of an encounter he had with a demon that was supposedly oppressing his daughter, Judy, and causing sickness and nausea. Once Bubeck was convinced that the problem was not psychosomatic but demonic, he decided that the best approach was to "work directly against these afflicting powers."[13]

After reading Scriptures which "speak of our great victory and the power of our Lord over all of Satan's kingdom,"[14] they prayed. Bubeck then recalls, "At this point I began to *command* for the powers of darkness afflicting her to come to manifestation. I *called them* before her faculties and *commanded* them to answer my questions."[15] He then recalls praying,

In the name of the Lord Jesus Christ, I *command Satan* and all wicked spirits who do not have specific assignment against Judy to leave our presence. We do not allow any interference or intrusion into our warfare against the powers of darkness afflicting Judy. I *command* all powers of darkness afflicting Judy to be bound aside. You may not work. You may not hurt her in any way. There is to be one-way traffic, out of Judy's life and to the place where the Lord Jesus Christ sends you. You may never return to afflict Judy. I *call you* before Judy's faculties. You *must answer* my questions by giving clear answers through her mind. You *may not speak* otherwise. I *want* no talk from you but answers to my questions. I *command* the chief power of darkness in charge of this affliction of fear, nausea, and all related problems to come to attention. I *call you to account* in the name of the Lord Jesus Christ. What is your name?[16]

---

confrontations with the forces of darkness. We will take a look at the Bible's teaching on exorcisms in Chapter 12.

[13] Mark I. Bubeck, *The Adversary: The Christian Versus Demon Activity* (Chicago: Moody Press, 1975), 120.

[14] Ibid.

[15] Ibid.

[16] Ibid., 120-121. Emphasis added to demonstrate the theology of "commanding" obedience from demons.

This was followed by a conversation with demons which revealed a supposed "hierarchy" of demonic powers responsible for this affliction. After being sufficiently convinced that the demons were fully exposed, Bubeck "proceeded to *command* their departure" with prayers like, "In the name of the Lord Jesus Christ, *I bind you* all together. *I bind* all workers and helpers together. . . . *I command* you to go where the Lord Jesus Christ sends you. *I command* you to go now."[17]

Rebuking the devil is presented as a quick and effective answer to temptation. When the Devil tempts you to sin, we are told to rebuke the demon of "lust," "alcohol," "depression," "homosexuality," "pornography," "worry," or "gossip." Deliverance from darkness or sin can be gained for family members when we rebuke the devil. The same theology that leads one to attempt to "bind Satan," also teaches that by rebuking the devil, we can cause him to flee or cower away from us. So it is not uncommon in Christian circles to hear pastors and teachers rebuke Satan and command him and his demons to leave or cease their activities. It is believed that if Jesus rebuked Satan and his demons (Mark 1:25; Matthew 17:18), we can also command Satan in Jesus' name and he will be obliged to obey our commands.

Is "rebuking Satan" mentioned in Scripture? Yes, it is. But not in a way favorable to the theology of modern spiritual warfare teachers.

2 Peter and False Teachers

Peter wrote his second epistle primarily to warn about the false teachers that would try to secretly introduce destructive heresies denying the Master (2:1-3). Peter wanted to prepare his readers to stand against the very real threat of wicked, ungodly men whose doctrines posed a grave threat to the truth and the health of the church.

In describing these men and their teachings, Peter reminds his readers that

---

[17] Ibid. 121-122. Emphasis added.

The Lord knows how to rescue the godly from temptation, and to keep the unrighteous under punishment for the day of judgment, and especially those who indulge the flesh in its corrupt desires and despise authority. Daring, self-willed, they do not tremble when *they revile angelic majesties*, whereas angels who are greater in might and power do not bring a reviling judgment against them before the Lord. (2:9-11)[18]

Like the devil, who is their father, these false teachers show their self-centered arrogance. Their self-willed presumption and their reckless daring are seen in the fact that "they do not tremble when they *revile angelic majesties*" (v. 10). The word translated "revile" in the passage is "*blasphemeo*," from which we get our English word blaspheme. It means "to slander" or to "speak lightly or profanely of sacred things." The "angelic majesties" in this context are demons (cf. Jude 8). They are are "majesties"[19] in the sense that they possess a transcendent, supernatural being beyond that of humans.[20]

These false teachers, in their brash rejection of authority, presumed they were greater than fallen angels, able to control them, and so spoke reviling evil of them. These false teachers are contrasted with angels, who are far greater in power and might than a mere man. Yet, even though the righteous and holy angels do not rebuke, revile, and speak evil of Satan and his demons, false teachers do! They recklessly presume that they, mere fallen men, have power and authority over demons to command and control them. Sound familiar?

Peter goes on to describe these reckless false teachers as being "like unreasoning animals, born as creatures of instinct to be captured and killed, *reviling* where they have no knowledge." He assures us that they "will in the destruction of those creatures also be

---

[18] Emphasis added.
[19] The Greek word is *doxa* which means "glories."
[20] John MacArthur, *The MacArthur New Testament Commentary: 2 Peter & Jude* (Chicago: Moody Press, 2005), 98.

destroyed" (2:12). They speak evil of things of which they are ignorant.

Jude Agrees

Like Peter, Jude wrote to warn Christians about false teachers. Those false teachers that Peter had warned *would* come into the church, Jude notes, *had* come into the church (v. 4). Jude's description of these false teachers is similar to Peter's. In fact, Jude notes the same rejection of authority and reviling of angelic majesties that Peter warned about, saying,

> Yet in the same way these men, also by dreaming, defile the flesh, and reject authority, and *revile angelic majesties*. But Michael the archangel, when he disputed with the devil and argued about the body of Moses, did not dare pronounce against him a railing judgment, but said, "The Lord rebuke you!" But these men revile the things which they do not understand; and the things which they know by instinct, like unreasoning animals, by these things they are destroyed (Jude 8-10).[21]

Like Peter, Jude notes the rejection of authority which is endemic among false teachers. Again, we see their arrogant presumption demonstrated when they "revile angelic majesties." Jude uses the very same words as Peter to describe this act of rebuking, reviling, and speaking evil of fallen angels.[22]

Though Peter noted that holy angels, even from their exalted, mighty, and glorious position, do not revile their fallen counterparts, Jude offers a very concrete example in Michael, the archangel. Michael apparently was given charge over the body of Moses (Deuteronomy 34:5-6). If not for this passage in Jude, we would not know there was a contention between Michael and Satan over Moses' body. Jude notes that when this happened, Michael "did not dare to

---

[21] Emphasis added.

[22] "Although it is possible to interpret the word [*doxa*, 'glories' or 'majesties'] as a reference to God's majesty, the translation 'angelic majesties' is best in light of the parallel passage in Peter's epistle" (MacArthur, 174).

bring a railing judgment" against Satan. Instead, Michael knew that only the Sovereign Lord was in a position to rebuke, control, or command Satan. Michael submitted to the Lord rather than dare to rebuke Satan and revile him.

Who Do You Think You Are?

What God's highest holy angel would not dare to do, sinful, fallen men presume the authority to do. It is unthinkable. I have been in the presence of Christians who boldly declare, "Satan, I rebuke you in the name of Jesus," and I wonder, "Who do you think you are?" Rebuking, commanding, or ridiculing the devil are not tools of effective spiritual warfare; they are marks of prideful, arrogant, self-willed false teachers. If you listen to false teachers like Benny Hinn, Kenneth Copeland, Robert Tilton, and Jesse Duplantis, you will hear them constantly ridicule, rebuke, and taunt the devil. These men are not masters in the art of spiritual warfare; they are unreasoning beasts reviling in their ignorance, rushing headlong into error and judgment.

Does that mean that every Christian who has uttered such phrases is a false teacher? No, certainly not. Some people are simply mistaken about the nature of spiritual warfare and the nature of the enemy. They are acting out of ignorance. As Peter says, they are "reviling where they have no knowledge." Jude says they "revile the things which they do not understand." I believe that explains much of the misguided attempts at confronting forces of darkness. "This is an example of ignorance of God's Word leading to wrong practice in the area of spiritual warfare."[23]

Since we have not one, but two stern warnings against such practices, we have to ask, "Why would anyone want to engage in this behavior? What makes us think we have more might, more power, than Michael the archangel?"

---

[23] Thomas Ice and Robert Dean, *A Holy Rebellion: The Church's New Preoccupation with the Demonic* (Eugene: Harvest House Publishers, 1990), 168.

More Problems to Note

Apart from the fact that we are warned about such bold, brash confrontation with fallen angels, there are a number of other problems with this practice.

First, we don't have a single positive example of such practices in the early church. In fact, we do have a negative example of some who presumed such authority, but without divine warrant - the sons of Sceva in Acts 19:11-20. Luke records this episode so that none would arrogantly assume that the extraordinary miracles performed by Paul (like exorcisms - Acts 19:11) were the norm for every believer. Aside from Jesus and the apostles, we do not have any record of such bold confrontation of demonic powers being practiced in the church.

In fact, Paul himself did not model this type of handling of demonic powers when he was afflicted by his thorn in the flesh, a messenger of Satan sent to torment him (2 Corinthians 12:7-10). Paul did not bind the devil, rebuke the satanic emissary, cast Satan down, revile him, or otherwise confront the spirit behind the thorn. Yet this type of behavior is precisely what is advocated by Bubeck, Anderson, and others.

The apostolic example is of resisting the devil (1 Peter 5:9) and standing (Ephesians 6:10-14), not binding and rebuking. Not only does the New Testament not provide us any examples of Christians handling the devil in this manner, there is not even a single command or instruction on rebuking the devil. The emphasis of the epistles rests on the victory which has already been won at Calvary, resisting, and standing.

Second, this produces a misdirected focus. God should be the focus of our prayers, not devils. It does not even seem wise that we should direct our attention and prayers toward commanding, rebuking, or addressing demons. The believer's focus in prayer should be the glories of God, the nature of Christ, and the work of the Triune God in His self-glorification. This approach to spiritual warfare places the emphasis on the devil and his activities - something I am sure he enjoys.

We do not see similar emphasis and misdirected focus in the writings of the apostles or in the life of the early church. In all the recorded prayers of the apostles and the early Christians, we do not find a single example of rebuking Satan or demons.

Third, far too much is made of the power of Satan and the authority of the believer. Satan is a defeated foe (Hebrews 2:14-15; Colossians 2:15). This is not to suggest that we should not take the threat he presents seriously. We should (1 Peter 5:8-9). However, modern spiritual warfare teachers give him far too much credit. Further, they make far too much out of the "authority" that comes with being a believer. Though we are seated with Christ in heavenly places (Ephesians 2:6), that positional privilege does not give us miracle-working power equivalent to Jesus and the apostles.

Fourth, the God-given method for dealing with temptation is to take the way of escape which God provides (1 Corinthians 10:13), not rebuking the demon assumed to be behind the temptation. There is no quick fix for temptation. We must resist it, endure it, and flee from it. We grow in holiness as we learn to yield our members as instruments of righteousness and not to sin (Romans 6:12-23). Rebuking a devil does not make temptation go away. We are tempted by our flesh and led astray through our lusts (James 1:14). The teaching on "rebuking Satan" as a means of sanctification and victorious Christian living thwarts God's sanctification process. This errant theology teaches that victory over temptation is achieved through a correct verbal formula (such as, "I bind/rebuke you Satan, in the name of Jesus") rather than through correct moral choices. Biblically, victory is enjoyed by denying the flesh, not defeating the devil. Rather than viewing temptation as something to be dealt with by making wise moral choices, this teaching adopts a ritualistic response more in keeping with a mystical/magical worldview.

We dare not rebuke demons! This is a completely unnecessary, unbiblical, and unwise practice. We are not commanded to wage the truth war in this fashion. Like the practices of binding Satan, praying hedges, and renouncing curses, rebuking demons is a tool that God has not put in our arsenal. It is a completely man-made tactic which appeals to the pride of our flesh. Satan does not fear our useless incantations. Let's abandon them and exchange them for the proclamation of the truth!

9

Carnal Weapons: Spiritual Mapping

What do you get when Christians abandon Scripture as the sole sufficient guide for faith and practice, and launch out to attack the enemy in their own strength and wisdom? You get "spiritual mapping" and the practice of "Strategic-Level Spiritual Warfare." It is difficult to point to a more disastrous, dangerous, and destructive practice in modern spiritual warfare theology than that of engaging "territorial spirits."

The practice we will examine in this chapter is sometimes referred to as "Spiritual Mapping," "Strategic-Level Spiritual Warfare," "Territorial Spirits," or even just "Mapping." This may be the fastest-growing approach to evangelism in the church today. This practice is not limited to charismatic churches and has become commonplace both in the United States and on the foreign mission field.

The Practice Defined and Described

Strategic-Level Spiritual Warfare (SLSW) is the practice of engaging in intercessory prayer for different geographical locations to overcome and dislodge supposed demonic strongholds in those locations. SLSW teaches that there is an extensive demonic hierarchy over geographical areas which must be actively overcome through intercessory prayer and repentance before effective gospel ministry will be possible. According to SLSW practitioners, these demons must be confronted, bound, and removed before the gospel can effectively penetrate. These regional and geographic demons are referred to as "territorial spirits." It is believed that territorial spirits become entrenched in different regions because of sins committed

115

there. John Dawson has advocated "identificational repentance," which is the practice of discovering the sin or guilt which has given the demonic realm a foothold in the area and repenting of that sin in order to break the demon's grip.

"Mapping" is the related practice of determining the exact boundaries of territorial spirits assigned to different regions, nations, or cities. It is believed that the demons must be specifically identified and named in order to pray, bind, and exorcise them effectively. This practice has been made popular by George Otis, Jr., famous for his *Transformations* videos. Like Otis, John Dawson encourages people to research their city's history in order to identify the particular blend of demonic forces which may be keeping people in spiritual darkness.

The teachings of John Dawson and George Otis have been promoted by C. Peter Wagner, who from 1991 to 1999 taught at Fuller Theological Seminary School of World Mission. As a result of Wagner's influential position, hundreds of pastors, leaders, and missionaries were exposed to this practice during that time.[1]

The practice was virtually unheard of until the early 1980s, after a series of city-wide gospel campaigns in Latin America met with unexpected success. That success was attributed by the evangelists to days spent in prayer, wrestling against the powers of darkness.[2] A movement was born! Thanks to the charismatic influence of C. Peter Wagner, this teaching gained a full head of steam and wide acceptance. In 1993 Wagner published a book titled, *Breaking Strongholds In Your City: How to Use Spiritual Mapping to Make Your Prayers More Strategic, Effective and Targeted* (Regal Publishers), in which he confessed that he had never heard of the term "spiritual mapping" until 1990. He admitted that it was an entirely new practice, but was "one of the most important things the Spirit is saying to the churches in the 1990s. . . ."[3]

---

[1] Other leaders in this movement include David Yonggi Cho, Cindy Jacobs, Dick Bernal, and Larry Lea. The A.D. 2000 United Prayer Track is the ministry currently headed by George Otis, Jr.

[2] http://www.plymouthbrethren.org/article/418

[3] C. Peter Wagner, *Breaking Strongholds in Your City: How To Use Spiritual Mapping To Make Your Prayers More Strategic, Effective and Targeted* (Ventura: Regal Books, 1993), 11-12.

Error abounds once it is believed that the Holy Spirit is saying something different today from what He said 2,000 years ago. One wonders how the church ever evangelized millions, penetrated unreached people groups, and survived until today without this supposedly vital practice.

According to advocates of SLSW, once the particular sins that have brought demonic power over a city or geographical region have been identified, they must be repented of and renounced. Identifying these "spirits" is often the result of personalized revelation from the Holy Spirit in prayer.[4] In some cases, advocates of SLSW teach that the names of demons over geographic regions should be discovered. According to Wagner,

> Another Latin American, Rita Cabezas, has done considerable research on the names of the highest levels of the hierarchy of Satan. I will not at this point describe her research methodology exce6pt to mention that the beginning stages were associated with her extensive psychological/deliverance practice and that it later evolved into receiving revelatory words of knowledge. She has discovered that directly under Satan are six worldwide principalities, named (allowing that this was done in Spanish) Damian, Asmodeo, Menguelesh, Arios, Beelzebub and Nosferasteus. Under each, she reports, are six governors over each nation. For example, those over Costa Rica are Shiebo, Quiebo, Ameneo, Mephistopheles, Nostradamus and Azazel. Those over the U.S.A. are Ralphes, Anoritho, Manchester, Apolion, Deviltook and one unnamed.[5]

---

[4] John Dawson, *Taking Our Cities For God: How To Break Spiritual Strongholds* (Lake Mary: Creation House, 1989), 154. Obviously I would take issue with anyone who teaches that God is revealing to the church today, information essential for the proclamation and success of the gospel.

[5] C. Peter Wagner and F. Douglas Pennoger, eds., *Wrestling with Dark Angels* (Ventura: Regal Books, 1990), pp. 84-85 as quoted in Thomas Ice & Robert Dean, Jr., *Overrun By Demons: The Church's New Preoccupation With The Demonic* (Eugene: Harvest House Publishers, 1990), 31.

Advocates of SLSW teach that knowing this information is essential to effective spiritual warfare and gospel ministry. They believe these demons should be researched, known by name, prayed against, bound, rebuked, and cast out by name through the unified prayers of God's people.

Biblical Support?

Most advocates of SLSW point to Daniel 10:13 and the reference to the "prince of Persia" as support for this teaching. A look at this passage in its context reveals that this veiled and scant reference does not support these practices at all.

Daniel was given a message which distressed him greatly. It was revealed to Daniel that the nation, in spite of their return from captivity, would be involved in a great conflict (10:1). Daniel was so distressed that he fasted and prayed for three weeks (v. 2). After three weeks, Daniel was visited by an angel[6] who revealed that

From the first day that you set your heart on understanding this and on humbling yourself before your God, your words were heard, and I have come in response to your words. But the prince of the kingdom of Persia was withstanding me for twenty-one days; then behold, Michael, one of the chief princes, came to help me, for I had been left there with the kings of Persia (10:13).

After the angelic messenger explained the vision and strengthened Daniel, he said,

Do you understand why I came to you? But I shall now return to fight against the prince of Persia; so I am going forth, and behold, the prince of Greece is about to come. However, I will tell you what is inscribed in the writing of

---

[6] Some people take this to be the pre-incarnate Christ, the Angel of the Lord, which I think is unlikely, since Christ would not need the assistance of Michael to defeat the prince of the Kingdom of Persia (10:13ff). On this occasion, God chose to use an angel to bring a message to Daniel. This was probably Gabriel, who earlier was used to bring a message to Daniel (see Daniel 8:15-17), though we cannot be sure.

truth. Yet there is no one who stands firmly with me against these forces except Michael your prince (10:21).

This passage offers us a glimpse into the warfare waged in the spiritual realm that Paul mentions in Ephesians 6. It is a very interesting passage of Scripture and from it we can draw the following conclusions:

First, there is a very real spiritual battle being waged of which we are, for the most part, completely oblivious.

Second, there was a demon or evil spirit assigned to Persia and to Greece, whose primary goal was to oppose the plan and purpose of God in regards to those nations, and to oppose the people of God in those nations.[7]

Beyond that, we are not told anything. We are not told that nations today have the same type of "prince." We are not told what the names of the princes of Persia and Greece were. We are not told what the names of the princes of other nations are today. All we can conclude is that there was an evil spiritual force behind the rulers of the nations of Persia and Greece, probably in the same way that Satan was really the influence behind the King of Tyre (Ezekiel 28:11-19) and the king of Babylon (Isaiah 14:3-21).

Did Daniel pray against these evil spirits? Did he even know this resistance to Gabriel was taking place? Did Daniel cast down, bind, rebuke, or exorcise these spirits? Did this battle involve any humans whatsoever? The answer to all these questions is no. Daniel was not even asked to pray for Gabriel in his return mission to fight again with the prince of Persia (Daniel 10:20-21). The conflict was fought by God through His angels in the heavenlies. It seems that Daniel was completely unaware of the reality of that spiritual conflict. The Lord did not reveal to Daniel the name of these evil demonic spirits. One would think that if this was necessary for victory, God would have told the great prophet Daniel, but no such directive or divine revelation was given.

---

[7] In the same sense, Michael, the archangel, is called a prince of Israel in Daniel 12:1. "Now at that time Michael, the great prince who stands guard over the sons of your people, will arise." Michael has a special relationship to Israel (Daniel 10:21; Jude 9).

If this passage does not teach us to name and pray against demonic powers attached to various geographical locations, then what does it teach us? It teaches us that the battle is real and God is fighting it. It teaches us that there are real demonic forces which oppose, resist, and seek the ruin of the people of God. It teaches us that God's holy angels eventually triumph in God's power over all His enemies. Further, it teaches us that Satan is the "god of this world"[8] and that the whole world, including political rulers, and nations, lies under his sway.[9] None of this should surprise us since we can glean the same information from other places in Scripture.

Other Problems

The practice of spiritual mapping and naming territorial spirits is fraught with problems.

First, it is without precedent or prescription in Scripture. The Bible is silent about this. You will read your New Testament in vain looking for references to apostles or Christians engaged in spiritual mapping. The practice was not even invented until around 1990. It clearly cannot find its genesis in Scripture, or it would have been a practice of the church since the first century.

Paul never had to name demons, spiritually map cities, or engage in identificational repentance prior to taking the gospel into a new city. Oh, if only the Apostle had known this principle, he might have been successful in his endeavors! If only he had been as spiritual and wise as John Dawson and C. Peter Wagner! Imagine what Jesus and the apostles could have accomplished if they had taken their cues from these men! There is not a single example or instruction in all of the Bible to support this nonsense. Not one!

Second, this practice is an entirely man-made, carnal, fleshly activity. We continually return to the principle stated near the beginning of this book, that we must let the Scriptures inform our methods of spiritual warfare. Our Commander-In-Chief has given us all the instructions and information necessary to wage this warfare.

---

[8] 2 Corinthians 4:3-4.
[9] 1 John 5:19.

120

He has not left us without essential information. We are to wage the war in the manner He has prescribed, not in a manner invented by some teacher of questionable theology nineteen centuries after the Apostles.

The weapons of true spiritual warfare are not man-made and carnal (2 Corinthians 10:3-5), but spiritual mapping is. It is fleshly. It is entirely of human origin, a goofy invention of charismatic teachers who think God is currently revealing a practice for the church of today that He has withheld from His people for nearly 2000 years.

To adopt this practice is to abandon the God-ordained means of waging warfare - truth. It is to trade in a nuclear weapon for a cardboard sword. As with all man-made methods and fads, spiritual mapping will run its course, the books advocating it will fall out of print, and the teachers teaching it will pass from the scene. Unfortunately, another dangerous and disastrous, man-made fad will quickly take its place, deceiving and distracting believers from the real battle over truth.

A third problem concerns the method by which information of the spiritual realm is gathered. Since the Bible is completely silent on the subject of the names of individual demons, the information about this must be gleaned from some source *outside* of Scripture. Please don't miss the obvious implication! We are told that knowing these demon's names, hierarchy, and geographical assignment is *essential* to effective spiritual warfare and the unhindered spread of the gospel. Yet Scripture *does not* reveal that information. What does that tell you about Scripture? It must be insufficient. God has not revealed all that we need to know. We must go outside the Bible to get the good stuff, the information necessary for effective gospel ministry! It is this completely inadequate view of Scripture that runs rampant in Charismatic circles and among advocates of this practice.

Take as an example the quote from Wagner cited above about the methods of Rita Cabezas who has supposedly "done considerable research on the names of the highest levels of the hierarchy of Satan"[10] in order to find out that under Satan were "six

---

[10] *Wrestling*, p. 84-85.

121

worldwide principalities."[11] Wagner indicates that this knowledge was gleaned in two ways: first, "extensive psychological/deliverance practice"[12] and later, "receiving revelatory words of knowledge." That means Cabezas gleaned some information from her direct interaction with demons during deliverance sessions (exorcisms), and other information was revealed by God personally to her through direct revelation.

Do we really think that we can trust a demon to give reliable information when asked for it? I have read books by Rebecca Brown and Mike Warnke in which they have claimed that when a demon is commanded to speak the truth and only the truth in the name of Jesus Christ the Son of God, they are bound and obligated to tell the truth. Really? How do we know that? Is there a verse somewhere in Scripture that tells us that? Does Scripture teach that we should be interviewing demon-possessed people in order to obtain knowledge about the satanic hierarchy? Certainly not! Besides, should we really be trusting information that comes from the prince of darkness, the father of lies (John 8:44)?

Christians should not base their theology, prayers, and spiritual warfare practices on information gleaned from the enemy. We can't trust it and should not even be seeking it! This is total nonsense!

It means nothing to advocates of spiritual mapping to point out that Scripture is silent on the subject and the apostles never prescribed nor practiced this method of spiritual warfare. To them, the Scriptures only serve to support what they receive through private revelation. Sure, the Bible does not give us the names of the six worldwide principalities of the satanic hierarchy, but God personally revealed that to someone. According to C. Peter Wagner, this is what "the Spirit is saying to the churches in the 1990s. . . ."[13] Apparently, it is different from what the Spirit revealed to the church of the first century, and different from what the Spirit has been revealing to the churches for the last 1900 years.

---

[11] Ibid.

[12] Wagner would not comment on her methodology, but the mention of psychological practices makes one wonder if hypnotism was involved.

[13] *Breaking Strongholds in Your City*, 11-12.

This is what you get when you abandon Scripture as the sole sufficient source of information and revelation. Pandora's box is opened and out slithers an endless parade of aberrant practices and heresies. False teaching is justified with, "The Lord is revealing this to me/us/the church by a word of knowledge. This is what God is showing us today. We have a fresh word from God for our generation." Of course that implies that Scripture is the stale word, for a prior generation, a prior church, but is not really necessary for us. If God is revealing this type of essential information to us today, then really, there is no need for Scripture at all. I see this as an all-or-nothing issue.

With this practice, "Christians" willingly set aside the more sure Word of God (2 Peter 1:19) in favor of personalized subjective revelation and even the testimony of demons! They affirm through this methodology that Scripture is not sufficient to equip us for the warfare, but the testimony of demons given during exorcisms, or personal subjective revelations from God will do the trick. That is tragic on so many levels!

A biblical view of spiritual warfare does not treat Scripture as an appendix to my personal revelations and the testimony of demons, but as the only sufficient source of truth by which the war is waged. Our Commander-in-Chief has not left us without adequate information, and He is not changing the battle plan in the middle of the war.

If God is revealing this information to these modern-day spiritual warfare "experts," should we not be writing this in the back of our Bibles as additional revelation? Should it not be published with each Bible as the 67th book? Certainly, if this is what the Spirit is speaking to the church today, it is just as authoritative and relevant - dare I say, more so - than what the Spirit said to the church of the first century. After all, this is supposedly essential to the health and success of the church!

Fourth, this methodology diminishes the power and authority of the gospel. This should come as no surprise. If the Bible itself is treated as less credible than personal revelation and the words of demons, it should come as no shock that the gospel should be undermined as well.

We are told that, prior to evangelizing a city, a region, or a nation, the area must be researched, repented for, and prayed for in a unified fashion. We are told that specific demonic strongholds and spirits, and even the demons themselves, must be addressed, rebuked, exorcised and cast down in order to break the hold of Satan and make a way for the gospel. Not according to the Apostle Paul. The gospel itself is the "power of God unto salvation" (Romans 1:16). It needs no help. God is sovereign and will save whomever He wants, whenever He wants, and Satan does not, and cannot, stand in the way of God redeeming His elect.

The preaching of the Cross is attended by the Spirit of God (1 Thessalonians 1:5), and is powerful to the saving of the soul, demonic strongholds and satanic activity not withstanding. One thing and one thing only is necessary for God to redeem a sinner: the preaching of the gospel. This is why Paul devoted his life to that end (Acts 20:20-24).

The preaching of the gospel does not need our research into a city's sins and history. It does not need our "identificational repentance," our spiritual mapping, prayer walks, naming of territorial spirits, or discovery of Satan's hierarchy. If the success of the gospel depended on such fleshly, carnal, man-made activities, God would have revealed it in Scripture through the Apostles.

The gospel spread from Jerusalem (Acts 1) to the farthest reaches of the Roman empire (Romans 15:17-25) in only thirty years. How did it do this without prayer walks, spiritual mapping, and praying through demonic strongholds? How did the Apostles plant churches in idolatrous, demonic, fleshly, sinful cities like Corinth and Athens without identifying the six worldwide principalities and the names of demons supposedly assigned to oppress those regions? They believed that people would be born again by the Spirit-empowered declaration of the gospel. The gospel causes people to be born again, and the entrance of the gospel breaks the powers of darkness and delivers captives from the kingdom of Satan (Colossians 1:13-14).

The gospel does not need the implementation of man-made spiritual warfare strategies for its success. It does not require that we glean intelligence from demons and pray accordingly. The power of the gospel resides in the will of the Trinity to bring redemption to God's elect through the preaching of it. This methodology makes the success of evangelism dependent upon human ingenuity and activity rather than the sovereignty and power of God. This diminishes the power of the gospel.

Fifth, and I have saved this for last, it is just a silly practice. Let's accept for a moment that everything that SLSW and spiritual mapping advocates claim is true. Don't you think that Satan would just shuffle his hierarchy around every few weeks to keep us off balance? If knowing the names and territories of demons gives us the ability to bring down Satanic strongholds, don't you think that after we had interviewed enough demons and received enough words of knowledge, Satan would just reassign his minions?

If the demon assigned to Kootenai, the city in which I pastor a church, is named "Luciferious,"[14] and the success of evangelism in our city depended on naming and praying specifically against this demon, then once we found that out, don't you think Satan would just give the demon of Ponderay (a neighboring city) control over Kootenai, and reassign Luciferious to Ponderay? Then we would be back at square one! He would keep us forever guessing, chasing shadows, trying to hit a moving target. Then we would have to interview more demons and get more words of knowledge to find the name of the new demon ruler assigned to Kootenai. Minutes later, he would be reassigned and we would be back at the beginning.

If we have identified these spiritual strongholds, named them by name, cast them down, rebuked them, and exorcised them, then why after twenty years of this superior knowledge from God have we gained no ground? Should not the named and mapped regions be filled with the gospel, sound doctrine, and good churches? Yet can anyone name a single city in which this nonsense has been employed which has experienced dramatic revival and gospel renewal? Seattle,

---

[14] I am just picking a demon-sounding name out of the air for this!

125

San Francisco, Miami and Minneapolis are all still in the clutches of the evil one.

Nothing but a Distraction

Satan is content if Christians focus their time, attention, efforts, and prayers on things that accomplish nothing. He is delighted if we use every man-made, silly convention under the sun to fight him. Provided Christians are not resting in the sufficiency of Scripture (truth), fighting the war against his lies with the truth (2 Corinthians 10:3-5), and proclaiming the gospel of truth, his kingdom can advance.

Well meaning, but deceived, Christians have bought his lie that Scripture is not sufficient. He has thus removed from the church, it's one, infinitely powerful weapon. He has distracted the soldiers with goofy games and silly strategies that are powerless. They have the appearance of real warfare, but the substance of a shadow. They are illusions and distractions.

The one true war - the truth war - wages on. The church has laid aside truth and embraced mysticism. Our armory has been exchanged for carnal weapons of man's making and man's devising. The word of God takes a back seat to the testimony of demons. That is the sad state of modern evangelicalism and its view of spiritual warfare. Spiritual mapping and naming demons is just one manifestation of it.

Test all things, and hold fast to that which is true!

Part 3:
Explaining Biblical
Perspectives

10

Can a Christian Be Demon-Possessed?

No discussion of spiritual warfare would be complete without addressing the issue of whether or not a Christian can be demon-possessed. How one answers this question will, to a large extent, determine their approach to spiritual warfare. It will determine what type of pastoral counsel one is expected to give or receive. It will determine the way in which a believer battles against the world, the flesh, and the devil.

Entire ministries have been founded for the purpose of exorcising demons from Christians and teaching Christians how to exorcise demons from others. It will be no surprise to discover that believing a Christian can be demon-possessed fits nicely in the broader theology of spiritual warfare I have been critiquing in the previous chapters. I do not believe that it fits at all with a biblical view of spiritual warfare.

In this chapter I'll answer the arguments used to support the doctrine that Christians are subject to demon possession. The subject of exorcisms is a different, yet related, topic that I will examine in a later chapter.

The Two Views

Can a Christian be indwelt and controlled by a demon?

Some would answer that question with "yes," though they would not necessarily like the phrase "demon-possessed" and would instead prefer the term "demonized." They would argue that while a believer cannot be "owned" by a demon,[1] he or she can be indwelt and controlled by a demon. Those who believe that a demon

---

[1] Since, technically, Satan cannot own anything, they would argue that a believer, while belonging to God, can be indwelt and controlled by Satan. This ends up being a semantic distinction that makes little difference in the end.

can inhabit a Christian also believe that the remedy for such indwelling and control is an exorcism.

Others would answer the question with "no." They would argue that a demon cannot indwell a believer because a believer is indwelt by the Holy Spirit. They affirm that a demon can attack a believer, deceive a believer, tempt a believer, and even oppress (both physically and spiritually) a true believer. Notice that these are all activities external to the spirit/soul of the believer. Those who believe that a demon cannot indwell a Christian would promote resistance, not exorcism, as the proper method for dealing with satanic attack.

What Is Demon Possession?

We need to begin by defining some terms. Ice and Dean offer a helpful summary of the New Testament usage of the terms for demon possession:

The New Testament uses more than one term to refer to demon possession. First is the Greek word daimonizomai, which is a participial form of the more commonly used noun for demon (daimonion). Daimonizomai is usually translated "to be possessed by a demon," or when it is used to describe a person in that condition, it is rendered "demoniac." The word is used 13 times,[2] all in the Gospels, and is usually referred to by the English expression "to be demonized."

The second term in the Greek is "daimonion echein," "to have a demon." This phrase is used eight times in Matthew, Luke, and John.[3] The Greek grammar conveys the idea that the subject is characterized by having a demon indwell him. . . . "Demonized" and "to have a demon" are used in Scripture of only one extreme: to be inwardly controlled by an indwelling demon. They are never used to describe a case involving anything less. For example, these terms never describe Satan's activities of accusation, temptation,

---

[2] Matthew 4:24; 8:16, 28, 33; 9:32; 12:22; 15:22; Mark 1:32; 5:15, 16, 18; Luke 8:36; John 10:21.
[3] Matthew 11:18; Luke 7:33; 8:27; John 7:20; 8:48, 49 ("to not have a demon"), 52; 10:20.

deception, or persecution; they describe only the extreme case of being inwardly controlled by a demon.[4]

Those who argue that a Christian can be demonized seek to distinguish between being "owned" by a demon (possessed) and simply being "controlled by a demon at various levels." In contrast to Ice and Dean, Fred Dickason writes,

> "*Diamonizomenos*" does not mean "owned by a demon," but simply "demonized." This basically describes the condition of a person who is inhabited by a demon or demons and is in various degrees under control with various effects. The idea of ownership is foreign to the New Testament word and its usage. Satan and his demons own nothing. God owns them.[5]

Those who believe that a Christian can be demonized make no substantial distinction between being oppressed by a demon and being possessed by a demon. Someone tempted, attacked, influenced from without is, in their view, "demonized." So too is the one indwelt by a demon. It is a matter of degree.

Those who deny that a Christian can be demon-possessed would draw a sharp distinction between a demon indwelling a person from within and a demon attacking, tempting, or oppressing a person from without. While we agree that a demon can attack a believer from without, we deny that a demon could control a believer from within.

By "demon-possessed," we mean indwelt and controlled by a demon. It is obvious that a demon cannot own a person, but they can indwell people and animals, and it is to this we refer when we use the term "demon possession." The terms used in Scripture for a person who is "demonized" describe the extreme of being controlled by a demon. The question remains, "Does Scripture teach that this can be true of a believer?"

---

[4] Thomas Ice and Robert Dean, Jr. , *Overrun By Demons: The Church's New Preoccupation With The Demonic* (Eugene: Harvest House, 1990), 116, 118.

[5] Thomas B. White, *The Believer's Guide To Spiritual Warfare* (Ann Arbor: Servant Publications, 1990), 43.

This is no small distinction! Upon this issue a large amount of the teaching of modern spiritual warfare tactics rests. If believers are just as susceptible to all the influences of Satan and his control as unbelievers, then Christians need to have Satan's influence removed (exorcised) from them. Our standing in Christ is no more secure from the devil than that of an unbeliever. In fact, we are just as open to his attack and control as the rankest pagan.

The Danger of Experience-Based Theology

We must be sure that our understanding of demon possession be based on the biblical data and not on experience or clinical research. The danger of building a theology on experience can be seen in the writings of late scholar Merrill F. Unger.

In his book *Biblical Demonology*, published originally in 1952, Unger emphatically declared that "to demon possession only unbelievers are exposed."[6] Unger later admitted that this assertion "was based on the assumption that an evil spirit could not indwell the redeemed body together with the Holy Spirit."[7] By the time that Unger published his later book in 1971, he had changed his opinion. This change was not based on the text of Scripture, which he said "does not clearly settle the question."[8] Rather, Unger had received letters from Christian missionaries from all over the world who testified that they had witnessed "Christians" being demon possessed. Ungers's change in doctrine was not based on an exegetical study of the biblical text, but on experience.

Unger then went on to say,

. . . most Christians would hesitate to say that a believer can become demon-possessed. Such cases are rarely seen, if ever, in the United States. However, in lands where demon-energized idolatry has flourished unchecked by the gospel for ages, new believers who were delivered from demon possession have been known to become

---

[6] Merrill F. Unger, *Biblical Demonology: A Study Of The Spiritual Forces Behind The Present World Unrest* (Wheaton: Van Kampen Press, 1952), 100.

[7] Merrill F. Unger, *Demons In The World Today* (Wheaton: Tyndale Publishers, 1971), 116.

[8] Ibid.

repossessed when they return to their old idols. The testimonies of numerous missionaries in pagan areas support this evidence.[9]

Was Unger convinced by Scripture to change his position? No. He stated, "Everyday experience adds its testimony to that of Scripture that believers can be oppressed and enslaved by demon powers." Though Unger tries to get the biblical data to fit the experience, it is clear that experience is the determining factor and not Scripture. What type of experience does Unger have in mind? He quotes Hobart E. Freeman, a pastor: "In my personal experience, the majority of those for whom I have prayed for deliverance from occult oppression or subjection were Christians, including ministers and the wives of ministers."[10]

Another advocate of this position, Thomas White, writes, "I am aware that this position stirs the opposition of many who stand firm with the notion that the Holy Spirit and an evil spirit cannot cohabit the same vessel. But the bottom line is this: Scripture does not exclude the possibility, and clinical reality affirms it time and time again."[11] Once again, the silence of Scripture (supposedly) on the issue is interpreted in light of experience to support the belief that Christians can be indwelt and controlled by a demon.

Proof Texts to the Rescue!

Several biblical examples are typically cited to support the teaching that a believer can be possessed by a demon. We will examine each one to see if, indeed, the case can be made.

King Saul

King Saul is sometimes cited as an example of a believer that was possessed and/or controlled by a demon. 1 Samuel 16:14 records,

---

9 Ibid.
10 Ibid.
11 White, 45.

"Now the Spirit of the Lord departed from Saul, and an evil spirit from the Lord terrorized him."[12]

To cite King Saul requires quite a bit of question-begging. Those who use Saul as an example are *assuming* that Saul was a genuine believer. That is not an assumption that can remain unchallenged. Though at the time of his anointing as king, it *appears* that he was a man of God (1 Samuel 10), his subsequent behavior was inconsistent with that of a genuine believer (James 2:14).[13] The fact that he was chosen as king and used by God does not prove that he was a believer, since God used pagan kings such as Cyrus and Nebuchadnezzar as His chosen men to accomplish His various purposes.

Even if we grant for the sake of argument that Saul was a believer, it does not prove that a Christian *today* can be demon-possessed. The ministry of the Holy Spirit to believers in the Old Testament was remarkably different than today. The Holy Spirit did not permanently indwell believers in the Old Testament (Psalm 51:11).[14] That fact alone makes it impossible to draw any parallels between King Saul and a present day believer.

---

[12] Two other passages record the same thing. Both times Saul tried to pin David to the wall with his javelin. 1 Samuel 18:10–11: "Now it came about on the next day that **an evil spirit from God came mightily upon Saul**, and he raved in the midst of the house, while David was playing the harp with his hand, as usual; and a spear was in Saul's hand. Saul hurled the spear for he thought, 'I will pin David to the wall.' But David escaped from his presence twice." 1 Samuel 19:9–10: "Now there was **an evil spirit from the Lord on Saul** as he was sitting in his house with his spear in his hand, and David was playing the harp with his hand. Saul tried to pin David to the wall with the spear, but he slipped away out of Saul's presence, so that he stuck the spear into the wall. And David fled and escaped that night."

[13] Brent Grimsley and Elliot Miller, "Can A Christian Be Demonized?" *Christian Research Journal* (Summer 1993), 17-18.

[14] Some would argue that David's reference to the Spirit of God leaving him had only to do with his anointing as king over Israel and not the possibility that the Spirit of God would stop indwelling him. If that is the case, then David is only expressing his desire that God not remove His hand of blessing and favor from David. Those who hold this view of Psalm 51:11 and the ministry of the Holy Spirit under the Old Covenant, *still* affirm that a believer cannot be demon-possessed since the Holy Spirit indwelt believers in the same manner as under the New Covenant. They affirm that a demon and the Holy Spirit cannot indwell the same person. Regardless of whether you believe the Holy Spirit permanently indwelt Old Testament believers or not, we still cannot assume that Saul was one.

John Wimber and others would equate Saul's being tormented by a demon with demon possession. However, there are three reasons why the example of Saul is not a case of demon possession.[15]

First, the evil spirit is said to have been sent from God, not Satan. In the New Testament examples, there is no doubt that the evil spirits exorcised by Jesus were, in fact, sent and empowered by Satan.[16]

Second, the evil spirit that tormented Saul is said to leave when David played his harp,[17] and no demon is said in Scripture to depart at the playing of music. Instead, Jesus and the Apostles cast out the demons in the name of the Lord.

Third, and most significantly, the texts all say that the evil spirit came *upon* Saul or would depart from *upon* him. The text never says that an evil spirit *entered* Saul. The language of demon possession is that of entering into someone and not just coming upon someone. The language of these passages is what we would expect if it is describing an external attack which can happen to a believer.

Saul is offered as the clearest example from the Old Testament that a Christian can be demon-possessed. However, it cannot be assumed that Saul was a believer. Neither are the circumstances of his situation in any way parallel to the instances of demonization in the New Testament. After examining the case of Saul, I believe we can say that this case does not at all prove the point.

Daughter of Abraham

The Daughter of Abraham mentioned in Luke 13 is also cited as an example of a true believer being possessed by a demon. Luke 13:11 says, "And there was a woman who for eighteen years had had a sickness caused by a spirit; and she was bent double, and could not straighten up at all." After Jesus healed the woman, the Pharisees were indignant because it was the Sabbath. Jesus replied, "And this woman, a daughter of Abraham as she is, whom Satan has bound for eighteen long years, should she not have been released from this bond on the Sabbath day?" (Luke 13:16).

---

[15] Ice and Dean, 124-125.
[16] Matthew 12:22-29.
[17] 1 Samuel 16:23.

The fact that Jesus called her a "daughter of Abraham" is cited as proof that she was a believer. Her sickness caused by an evil spirit is seen as evidence that she was possessed (or demonized). Neil T. Anderson writes,

Verse 16 states that her physical disability was caused by satanic bondage. This woman was not an unbeliever. She was "a daughter of Abraham" (verse 16), a God-fearing woman of faith with a spiritual problem. . . . Notice that this woman wasn't protected from demonic control by being inside the synagogue. Neither the walls of a synagogue nor the walls of a church provide sanctuary from demonic influence. Admittedly, this event occurred before the cross. But it is an indication that demons can physically affect believers.[18]

Remember that physical affliction and total control are all part of being "demonized" in his view. According to Anderson, if a believer can be *afflicted*, he can be *controlled* and *indwelt*, since he makes no substantive distinction between the two. Anderson jumps from "spiritual problem" and "sickness caused by a spirit" to "demonic control." To him, it is all the same thing. Anderson's point that the walls of a synagogue or church could not protect one from demonic control is silly. Nobody believes that walls of a building can protect one from a spirit. However, I do believe that the work of the Sovereign God on the cross and His redemption of His people does provide sanctuary from demonic possession and control.

As with the case of King Saul, there is a bit of question-begging in the argument of Anderson. He is *assuming* that the "daughter of Abraham" was a genuine believer. Agreeing with Anderson, Fred Dickason contends that the woman was a true believer because (1) she worshiped at the synagogue, (2) she glorified God because of her healing, (3) the phrase "daughter of Abraham" implies salvation since Jesus seemed to suggest that she was a true Israelite with Abraham-like faith (a believer).[19]

---

[18] Neil T. Anderson, *The Bondage Breaker* (Eugene: Harvest House Publishers, 1990) 188.
[19] http://www.banner.org.uk/dev/dickch3.html

However, the fact that she worshiped at the synagogue is no sure indication she was a believer, since the Pharisees in the passage also worshiped at the synagogue and we would never consider them to be true believers. They were, in fact, opposing Jesus and His teachings. People can worship in a synagogue or a church and not be true believers. To borrow the language from Neil Anderson's silly analogy, being inside the walls of a synagogue or even a church do not indicate that one is a believer.

Second, there is no mention in the text that the woman became a believer, and even if she did, it would have been as a result of her deliverance rather than a cause of it.

Third, the phrase "daughter of Abraham" is no sure indication she was a believer. It is most likely simply used ethnically to indicate that she was a Jew. Right before His reference to her as a "daughter of Abraham," Jesus said, "You hypocrites, does not each of you on the Sabbath untie his ox or his donkey from the stall and lead him away to water him?" (Luke 13:15). Likely Jesus was emphasizing her ethnic relation to the Pharisees to show that their objection to His healing on the Sabbath was so utterly void of compassion for even this "daughter of Abraham" - their own fellow Israelite. They would show this compassion on the Sabbath to their animals, and here was a daughter of Abraham! Should she not, as a child of Abraham, receive at least as much compassion as their ox? Jesus used that phrase not to highlight her faith, but to show their hypocrisy and hard hearts.

Further, the text does not indicate that she was possessed. Luke notes that the cause of her disease was demonic. She was *crippled* by the spirit, but that is not the same as being *indwelt* and *controlled* by a demon. It is worth noting that Jesus did not cast the demon out, but rather cured her of the illness. In clear cases of demon possession, Jesus exorcised the demons. He did not do so in this case.

Judas Iscariot

Judas Iscariot is also offered as an example of a believer being demon-possessed. According to John Wimber,[20] Judas was a believer since he was one of the twelve disciples. We could never argue that Judas was not possessed by a demon since the Bible uses clear language to describe the fact that "Satan then entered into him" (John 13:27). It is clear that Judas was possessed by a demon.

However, it is equally clear that Judas was not a believer. In John 6:70-71, Jesus referred to Judas as "a devil." In John 13:10-11, Judas was singled out by Jesus as one whose sins were not forgiven, "because Judas was betraying Him."

It is a distortion of the clear teaching of Scripture to assert that Judas Iscariot was a believer when, in fact, Scripture makes it clear that even though he was among the Twelve, he was no true believer in Jesus. He was chosen by Jesus, not because he was a believer, but in order that the Scripture concerning His betrayal would be fulfilled.[21]

Peter

Peter is said to be a demon-possessed believer since, in Matthew 16:23, Jesus rebuked Peter saying, "Get behind Me, Satan!" It is argued that this indicates that Peter, no doubt a believer, was possessed by Satan.

If that is true, then it raises the question, "Why didn't Jesus exorcise the demon?" As with the other examples, this is an assumption, and as it turns out, not a good one. In Matthew 16, Satan's influence on Peter was from without, not within. Jesus' rebuke was intended to identify the source of Peter's thinking, just as Jesus had earlier identified the source of Peter's confession as being from "My Father Who is in Heaven."[22] Jesus was pointing out the spiritual entity that was influencing Peter's thinking. The text nowhere uses language that would indicate that Peter was possessed

---

[20] Ice and Dean, 125.
[21] John 13:18.
[22] Matthew 16:13-20.

and controlled by a demon. The language is consistent only with external influence.

Ananias and Sapphira

Ananias and Sapphira are also cited as examples of demon-possessed believers, since Peter said to them in Acts 5:3, "Why has Satan filled your heart to lie to the Holy Spirit?" It is *assumed* that since the heart of Ananias was filled, he was therefore possessed by Satan. Neil T. Anderson argues, "The word 'filled' in Acts 5:3 (pleroo) is the same word used in Ephesians 5:18: 'Be filled with the Spirit.' It is possible for the believer to be filled with satanic deception or filled by the Spirit. To whichever source you yield, by that source you shall be filled and controlled."[23]

Anderson draws a faulty conclusion from the use of *pleroo* by wrongly equating "filling" with "control." The word filled (*pleroo*) as used in the New Testament does not mean to "indwell" or to "control." In fact, this would be an impossible meaning for many of the usages of the word. For instance, Luke 3:5: "Every ravine will be *filled*, And every mountain and hill will be brought low; The crooked will become straight, And the rough roads smooth," or Luke 5:7: "So they signaled to their partners in the other boat for them to come and help them. And they came and *filled* both of the boats, so that they began to sink." You can see that the word "filled" does not necessarily mean "to be indwelt and controlled by." How is a ravine "controlled?" Did the fish indwell and "control" the boats?[24]

The phrase "filled your heart" can be taken in two ways. First, it could refer to demon possession - an interpretation I reject. Second, it could simply mean that Satan, the father of lies, has so influenced the heart of Ananias that his heart was filled with the desire to lie - such desire finding its source in Satan. This then would be another case of a demon influencing a Christian from without instead of from within.

---

[23] Anderson, 192.

[24] Consider also Luke 5:26; John 16:6; Acts 2:2; 3:10; 5:28; 19:29; 2 Cor. 7:4.

If we say that Ananias was indwelt and controlled by Satan, then it was not Ananias who lied, but Satan. If Ananias was under the control of Satan, then Satan is the one who spoke the lie, not Ananias. In that case, Satan, not Ananias, was responsible for the lie. Yet Peter says in the very next verse, "While it remained unsold, did it not remain your own? And after it was sold, was it not under your control? Why is it that you have conceived this deed in your heart? You have not lied to men but to God" (Acts 5:4).

Peter clearly believed that Ananias was responsible and not a demon. It is further evident from God's punishment of Ananias and Sapphira. He struck them dead for *their* sin (Acts 5:5, 10). If Ananias and Sapphira were demon-possessed, why didn't Peter simply exorcise the demons from them? Why were they punished for something that a demon did through them?

Satan influenced Ananias from outside, not inside. This is not an example of a believer being demon-possessed. Ananias and Sapphira were believers, but they were not possessed by a demon.

These are the most common examples put forth to show that Christians can be demon-possessed. Clearly, these do not make the case.

Other lines of argument are sometimes offered by advocates of this position. For instance, they take any teaching in the New Testament[25] on a believer standing against satanic forces and then reason that such teaching only makes sense if a Christian can be demonized (controlled or indwelt by a demon to various degrees). However, it does not follow that just because we are attacked outwardly by Satan, that he is therefore free and able to control a believer in the same way and to the same degree that he does an unbeliever. As we have seen, that is a teaching that is derived from experience and then imported into the text of Scripture.

Merrill Unger, who believed that Christians could be possessed, stated that Scripture "does not clearly settle the question."[26] Fred Dickason, though he agrees with Unger, is candid enough to admit,

---

[25] Ephesians 6; 1 Peter 5; 1 Corinthians 5; 2 Corinthians 12, etc.
[26] Unger, 116.

"We cannot conclusively say that the Bible clearly presents evidence that believers may be demonized."[27]

In order to make the case that a Christian can be demonized, advocates of that view must define "demonization" and "Christian" so broadly that those terms lose all meaning. I believe that the Bible is clear on the subject, and that every teaching in the New Testament about the position and privileges of a believer precludes the possibility of demon possession.

Not Possible

We might expect that an unbeliever could be possessed and controlled by a demon. An unbeliever belongs to the kingdom of darkness, belongs to the father of lies, and is under the sway of the wicked one.[28] These things are not true of a believer. In fact, the relationship of the believer to the world, the flesh, and the devil is so radically different from that of the unbeliever, that we are said to be entirely new creations.[29] The following lines of argument show that demon possession of a believer is completely impossible.

First, we have been delivered. Colossians 1:13 says that "He rescued us from the domain of darkness, and transferred us to the kingdom of His beloved Son."[30] We are no longer in the domain of Satan's kingdom. He can attack us, trick us, tempt us, and oppose us, but He cannot control or indwell us. We do not belong to Him.

Second, we are temples of the Living God. 1 Corinthians 6:19–20: "Or do you not know that your body is a temple of the Holy Spirit who is in you, whom you have from God, and that you are not your own? For you have been bought with a price: therefore glorify God in your body."

The assumption in Scripture is that one might have God dwelling in him, or Satan, but certainly not both. This is the foundation of Paul's argument in 2 Corinthians 6:14–16:

---

[27] C. Fred Dickason, *Demon Possession and the Christian: A New Perspective* (Chicago: Moody Press, 1987), p. 127, quoted in Brent Grimsley and Elliot Miller, "Can A Christian Be Demonized?" *Christian Research Journal* (Summer 1993), 17-18.

[28] Colossians 1:13; John 8:44; 1 John 5:19.

[29] 2 Corinthians 5:17.

[30] See also Acts 26:18.

Do not be bound together with unbelievers; for what partnership have righteousness and lawlessness, or what fellowship has light with darkness? Or what harmony has Christ with Belial, or what has a believer in common with an unbeliever? Or what agreement has the temple of God with idols? For we are the temple of the living God; just as God said, "I will dwell in them and walk among them; And I will be their God, and they shall be My people."

In this passage, the fact that we are the temple of God excludes such intimate fellowship with demons and/or idols. How then would God, who is mightier than Satan, allow a demon to reside with Him in a believer? It is unthinkable!

Third, John comforts his readers with the certainty that "You are from God, little children, and have overcome them; because greater is He who is in you than he who is in the world" (1 John 4:4). Those who say that a Christian can be demon-possessed would have to change this verse to read, "Greater is He who is in you than he who is in you." Clearly, God is in the believer and Satan is in the world. It cannot be the case that God is in the believer and Satan is in the believer.

Fourth, we are sealed and kept. Ephesians 1:13–14: "In Him, you also, after listening to the message of truth, the gospel of your salvation—having also believed, you were sealed in Him with the Holy Spirit of promise, who is given as a pledge of our inheritance, with a view to the redemption of God's own possession, to the praise of His glory." Since we belong to God, the Holy Spirit permanently indwells us and we are sealed by that same Spirit until the day of redemption. Because we are kept by God, the promise of Scripture is that the one in the world (Satan) does not touch us (1 John 5:18). The belief that a believer can be demon-possessed turns all these verses on their heads!

Fifth, there is a complete absence of instruction in the New Testament on how to deal with a demon-possessed believer. If, as is asserted, a Christian can be demon-possessed, we would not expect the New Testament epistles to be silent on how to handle such cases of demon possession. We would expect an abundance of information about how to prevent such possession and how to handle such possession. We would also expect numerous examples of possessed believers to fill the pages of the New Testament. We would expect that a church like that at Corinth, with its rampant sin and history of demon worship, would be subject to such demonic footholds and would receive instructions for dealing with demon-possessed believers. "For if deliverance is as important to victorious Christian living as its advocates would have us believe, we can rightly expect the New Testament to deal with it."[31] Yet we don't find any of this.

But if Christians can be possessed, then why do not the New Testament Epistles, those letters written specifically to teach believers how to live a victorious Christian life until the return of Christ, tell us that believers can be demon-possessed, or command us to cast out demons from Christians, or tell us how to otherwise deal with this problem? It is unthinkable that a subject as important as this one would not be dealt with in the Epistles. . . . if the Epistles gave instructions on how to cast out demons, then it would be clear that Christians could be demon-possessed. Therefore, since there are no instructions for dealing with demon-possessed Christians in the New Testament, and assuming that believers can be demon-possessed, then once again it is back to experience and trial and error as our teacher for functioning in this area.[32]

That is precisely where Unger, Anderson and others would have us get our theology - not from Scripture, but from trial and error experience. Consider what their position implies about Scripture. They believe that dealing with demon-possessed believers is essential to victorious Christian living. Yet there is not a word of such instruction in the Bible. We must conclude then that Scripture has not given us everything that we need for life and godliness. Instead, we

---

[31] Grimsley and Elliot, 19.
[32] Ice and Dean, 123.

must rely upon *their* methods and insights which are derived from experience, clinical research, and trial and error.

Sixth, the teaching of the New Testament for dealing with the devil is always the same: resist him.[33] "Never are believers said to respond to Satan or demons by casting them out, which is always the remedy in the New Testament for a demon-possessed person. Instead, for the believer the command is always to stand or resist, which is the counter to an external temptation by Satan and the demonic."[34]

What About the Experiences?

What are we to make of the various experiences that people have which seem to suggest that a Christian can be demon-possessed?

For starters, we begin by recognizing that our experiences must be interpreted in light of revelation from God and not the other way around. If we take the Bible's teachings as authoritative, then we are forced to find explanations for our experiences which harmonize with the clear teachings of Scripture. With this principle as our guiding concern, I believe there are at least three possible explanations for the experiences cited by Unger and others.

First, maybe these "believers" were not real believers at all. Unger says that "new believers who were delivered from demon possession have been known to become repossessed when they return to their old idols."[35] What?! Return to their idols? What type of conversion is it that results in a quick apostasy? It certainly is not a genuine regeneration by the Spirit of God. The real believers in Thessalonica did not turn back to their idols.[36] Those who turn back to their idols and leave Christ, show that they were never His to begin with.[37] They have never been set free from sin, self, and Satan and so

---

[33] 1 Peter 5:9; Ephesians 6:10-14; James 4:7.

[34] Thomas Ice, "Demon Possession and the New Clinical Deliverance," *Biblical Perspectives* May-June 1992, as quoted in Brent Grimsley and Elliot Miller, "Can A Christian Be Demonized?" *Christian Research Journal* (Summer 1993), 19.

[35] Unger, 116.

[36] 1 Thessalonians 1:10.

[37] 1 John 2:19.

we should not be surprised if they would be possessed sometime after *professing* a faith in Christ.

Second, these episodes may be satanic oppression and not possession. Perhaps in some circumstances they are genuine believers, who although not indwelt by a devil, have given such control over to Satan that they are oppressed to such a degree as to appear possessed. If a believer genuinely thinks that their sin, their sickness, their lack of victorious Christian living is the work of an indwelling and controlling demonic influence, and if they submit to this theology in their conduct, they can actually consciously yield their members to such an influence. The psychosomatic power of that belief in this unbiblical doctrine could end up yielding enough control to a demon that its oppression from without would end up looking like possession from within.

Third, it could be sheer demonic deception. Satan would love for Christians to think that he has more power than he does. If we lived in fear of him, constantly thinking that he indwelt us and controlled us, constantly seeking to exorcise Him out of believers, he would have the church chasing shadows. Satan benefits if our theology about him is wrong. He has a vested interest in deceiving believers about how he is to be handled. The enemy gains a victory when he is able to take Christians, by the thousands, out of the real conflict and get them engaged in an imaginary one with carnal weapons.

I believe that the experience-driven theology of Christian demon possession is a demonic deception. It is a deception that Satan has successfully fostered by possessing false converts and oppressing genuine ones, while undermining our confidence in the clear teaching of Scripture.

Can a Christian be demon-possessed? No. Definitely not. Nothing from Scripture or experience suggests otherwise.

11

Is Christ's Authority Ours?

Let's start with a game called "Spot the Flaw." Here's how we play: I will lay out an argument - a line of thinking - complete with conclusion and application. You try to spot the flaw in the argument. Are you ready? Here we go . . .

Jesus is God (John 1:1-14) and as God, He has all authority (Matthew 28:18). Jesus' authority extends not just over all physical created things (Mark 4:35-41), but in the spiritual realm as well (Ephesians 1:20-23). Jesus "disarmed the rulers and authorities" by triumphing over them on the cross (Colossians 2:15). Jesus is now seated at the right hand of the Father (Ephesians 1:20-21; Acts 2:33; Hebrews 1:13), a position of unlimited power and authority (Psalm 110:1). As a believer in Christ, I am blessed with every spiritual blessing in the Heavenly places in Christ (Ephesians 1:3), and have been "seated with Christ in the Heavenly places" (Ephesians 2:6). That position of authority that belongs to Christ is also mine by virtue of the fact that I am in Him. When I walk in Christ, I can use that authority to command demons, to exorcise demons, take back territory from Satan and set captives free, just like Jesus did.

Just as the apostles exercised their God-given authority over demons by aggressive spiritual warfare and exorcisms (Acts 5:12-16; 16:16-18), so should we. If I use my Heavenly Authority, I can likewise triumph over the spiritual realm and cast out, control, and command demons. Jesus is my model, my example. I can follow in His steps by using the authority that I have in Him. The demons will be subject to me so long as I use the power and authority granted to me by God.

How did you do? Did you spot the flaw? There is really no trick question here, though the flaw may not be readily apparent. Perhaps as you read through that, you got a bit uneasy at times. You agreed with it in the beginning, but as I continued through to the end, you got increasingly uncomfortable with the conclusions being drawn. Perhaps you got to the end and said, "Well, I know the wheels fell off that somewhere along the line, though I am not quite sure where."

If you have ever been exposed to the works and writings of the men I have critiqued in earlier chapters, men like Neil T. Anderson, Mark Bubeck, and Thomas B. White,[1] then the language and theology presented in the "Spot the Flaw" game will sound very familiar. This thinking is not merely alluded to from time to time, but is in fact, the foundation upon which an aggressive territorial approach to spiritual warfare is based. It is the bedrock of the modern deliverance ministry movement, which is characterized by the errant practices we have already examined.

Some Bold Assumptions

Neil T. Anderson has done more to make this thinking acceptable among rank and file non-charismatic evangelicals than any other modern writer. Anderson's entire approach to spiritual warfare is based upon the authority of the believer over the devil, which Anderson asserts is granted by Christ to His people. Anderson applies this authority to the issue of binding Satan saying,

God has granted us the authority to "bind what shall be bound in heaven" (Matthew 16:19; 18:18). In other words, we have the spiritual capacity to discern God's will and then, confident in the finished work of Christ, proclaim it in the spiritual realm. We have authority over demons as long as we remain strong in the Lord and operate in His strength (see Ephesians 6:10). . . . The effectiveness of binding the strongman (see Matthew 12:20 [sic]) is

---

[1] Others I have not yet mentioned would include Mike Warnke and Bob Larson and anyone from the Charismatic/Third Wave movement (John Wimber, John Arnott, Jack Deere, Jack Hayford and Rick Joyner) and the Word Faith Movement (Kenneth Copeland, Fred Price, Benny Hinn, Paul Crouch, etc.).

148

dependent upon the leading of the Holy Spirit and subject to the scope and limits of the written Word of God.[2]

As is typical of the deliverance movement, Anderson offers "how-to" help on finding freedom in Christ when he writes,

With this in mind, I usually begin the steps to freedom with a prayer similar to this: Dear heavenly Father. . . . I take my position with Christ, seated with Him in the heavenlies. Because all authority in heaven and on earth has been given to Him, I now claim that authority over all enemies of the Lord Jesus Christ in and around this room and especially (name).[3] You have told us that where two or three are gathered in Your name You are in our midst, and that whatever is bound on earth is bound in heaven. We agree that every evil spirit that is in or around (name) be bound to silence. . . . Now in the name of the Lord Jesus Christ I command you, Satan, and all your hosts to release (name) and remain bound and gagged so that (name) will be able to obey God.[4]

Likewise, Mark Bubeck begins his chapter titled, "Bold Confrontation May Be Needed,"[5] by quoting Mark 5:9: "And he asked him, 'What is thy name?' And he answered, saying, "My name is Legion: for we are many.'"[6] Bubeck then goes on to say,

This verse reveals that our Lord confronted wicked spirits boldly and demanded that they reveal their wicked

---

[2] "Twenty-Five Most Popular Questions," Freedom in Christ website, (http://www.ficm.org) as quoted by Elliot Miller, "The Bondage Maker: Examining the Message and Method of Neil T. Anderson, Part 2 - Spiritual Warfare and the Truth Encounter," *Christian Research Journal* , 21.2, 13. I have searched Freedom In Christ Ministry's website and been unable to find the "Twenty-Five Most Popular Questions" article.

[3] The reader is instructed to insert the name of the person for whom they are praying.

[4] Neil T. Anderson, *The Bondage Breaker* (Eugene, OR: Harvest House Publishers, 1990), 67-68. Quoted in Elliot Miller, "The Bondage Maker: Examining the Message and Method of Neil T. Anderson, Part 2 - Spiritual Warfare and the Truth Encounter," *Christian Research Journal* 21.2, 13-15.

[5] Mark I. Bubeck, *The Adversary: The Christian Versus Demon Activity* (Chicago: Moody Press), 115.

[6] King James Version.

presence and work in the lives of people. They, in turn, responded to His commands, and in so doing acknowledged His full authority over them.

Believers, united with the Lord Jesus Christ, in all of His person and work, *have the same authority* to claim and use that which our Lord used against wicked spirits."[7]

Bubeck goes on to quote J. A. MacMillan's book, *The Authority of the Believer*, calling it "one of the finest expositions upon the subject and basis of the believer's authority that I have ever read." [8] MacMillan, as quoted by Bubeck, writes,

It has been pointed out more than once in this study that *the authority* of which we are speaking is the *portion of every believer*. It is not a special gift imparted in answer to prayer, but the *inherent right of the child of God* because of his elevation with Christ to the right hand of the Father. He has become, through the rich mercy of God, an occupant of the Throne of the Lord, with *all that it implies in privilege and responsibility*.

This elevation took place potentially at the resurrection of the Lord and because of the believer's inclusion in Him. ... *It is ours simply to recognize the fact of this position*, and to take our place in humble acceptance, giving all the glory and honor to God.[9]

Bubeck then writes, "The believer's authority is truly a settled fact. . . .It remains for believers to act upon this powerful truth." He then chides "even the most devoted pastors and Christian leaders" who show "tragic temerity in any bold use of their authority in Christ," since they have "joined the ranks of those reticent to face any demonic power in a head-on confrontation."[10]

---

[7] Ibid. Emphasis mine.
[8] Ibid.
[9] Ibid. Emphasis mine.
[10] Ibid., 116.

For Bubeck, any hesitation to engage demonic forces in a power encounter such as exorcisms or demonic manifestations is "temerity" and cowardice. It never seems to occur to him that our hesitation might be theologically grounded on solid exegesis of Scripture and not merely an expression of cowardice and capitulation.

As you can see, the believer's equal authority to Christ is not just the hidden assumption of modern deliverance ministry leaders, it is the core teaching upon which all the other practices are founded. Practices such as binding Satan, rebuking Satan, praying hedges, and removing hexes all presume that the believer is vested with the type of authority described by Bubeck and Anderson. So before we address the issue of the legitimacy of practicing exorcisms, we need to analyze the authority-claim itself to see if it is justified.

A Matchless Messiah or a Model for Ministry?

It is assumed by modern deliverance ministry leaders and advocates that if something was done by Jesus, it was intended to be a model for us. Jesus confronting and speaking to a demon (Mark 5:8-9ff), His exorcisms of demons from a distance (Matthew 15:21-28) and in person (Matthew 17:14-18) are all treated as a model for modern deliverance techniques. It is *assumed* that if this characterized the ministry of Jesus and the Apostles, it should likewise characterize the gospel ministry of believers individually and the church corporately in all ages.

This is the Achilles heel of the argument I presented at the very beginning. It is an *assumption* which is sneaked into the reasoning without ever being explicitly stated or proved. Unfortunately for deliverance ministry advocates, this *assumption* is unfounded, unbiblical, and fails to account for what the Bible itself teaches about the unique person of Christ and His one-of-a-kind role in the redemptive plan of God.

When we examine the teaching of the gospels on the purpose of Jesus' signs, it becomes obvious that Jesus' confrontation with the demonic realm was not a model for us to follow, but proof of his unique Messianic claims. Many go astray by failing to understand

151

why Jesus encountered demons during His life on earth and why those events are recorded for us.[11]

The Reason Jesus Confronted Demons

A Messiah who could not conquer Satan would be no Messiah at all. The Jews expected the Messiah would demonstrate His power over Satan and his demons. After all, the very first prediction of a coming Redeemer promised this victory: "And I will put enmity between you and the woman, and between your seed and her seed; He shall bruise you on the head, and you shall bruise him on the heel" (Genesis 3:15). God promised that the Redeemer, Who would come through the seed of the woman, would crush the serpent's head dealing a fatal blow to his kingdom and authority. Only the long-awaited, long-promised Son of David, the Messiah, the King would exercise that authority over Satan's kingdom.

Matthew wrote his gospel for the purpose of proving that Jesus is that long-awaited fulfillment of Jewish expectation and promise. Matthew demonstrated that Jesus is the Son of David, the Messiah of Israel promised through the prophets. Many in Jesus' own day wrongly assumed that Jesus could not be the Messiah since the anticipated "Messianic Kingdom" had not arrived. Matthew shows us the reason for that delay of the Kingdom: the Jews rejected their King. Matthew's gospel builds as Jesus' miracles are recorded one right after another. These miracles are offered as proof of Jesus' claims to be not only the Son of God (John 5:36-37), but the Messiah (Luke 7:18-23).

Matthew repeatedly draws a connection between the signs Jesus performed and His claims to be the Son of David. For Matthew, the proof was in the pudding. The power over demons was evidence that Jesus was the Christ.

For instance, in Matthew 10:1-5 Jesus "summoned His twelve disciples and gave them authority over unclean spirits, to cast them

---

[11] Thomas Ice and Robert Dean, Jr. offer an excellent treatment of this subject in their book, *Overrun By Demons: The Church's New Preoccupation With The Demonic* (see chapter 6, "Invasion of the King" and chapter 7, "Strategies of the Enemy"). I am heavily indebted to Ice and Dean's work on this subject.

out, and to heal every kind of disease and every kind of sickness" (10:1).[12] This ability was given to accompany their preaching: "And as you go, preach, saying, 'The kingdom of Heaven is at hand'" (10:7). "What was the confirming evidence which would demonstrate to the lost sheep of the house of Israel that Jesus was the Messiah? The ability to heal and cast out demons."[13] Their ability was connected to their proclamation that the King had arrived and was in their midst. It was connected to the Messianic *claims* and *identity* of Jesus of Nazareth.

While still building toward the climactic conflict in chapter 12, chapter 11 records the inquiry of John the Baptist. While in prison, and facing death without seeing the dawn of the promised Messianic Kingdom, John doubted and sent to Jesus asking, "Are You the Expected One, or shall we look for someone else?" (11:1-3). Jesus responded by citing the signs He performed as proof of His Messianic claims saying, "Go and report to John what you hear and see: the blind receive sight and the lame walk, the lepers are cleansed and the deaf hear, the dead are raised up, and the poor have the gospel preached to them" (11:4-6). The parallel passage in Luke 7:21 includes the casting out of evil spirits among the signs that Jesus did as evidence of His claims.

In spite of this overwhelming evidence, the religious leaders of the nation attributed Jesus' works to the power of Satan. Matthew 12 records this climactic confrontation. Interestingly, this blasphemous attribution was in response to Jesus healing a demon-possessed man who was blind and mute (12:22). The crowds, amazed at Jesus' power over demons, began to say, "This man cannot be the Son of David, can He?" They started to get it, which is the very thing the Pharisees wanted to avoid. They did not want the people beginning to accept the notion that Jesus was the Messiah.

In the face of overwhelming evidence, the Pharisees had two choices: one, admit Jesus was the Messiah and humbly bow before

---

[12] Lest we mistakenly think that this same authority is given to all disciples in every age, Matthew specifically names the twelve for us (v. 2-4), as if to emphasize the restricted nature of this ability.

[13] Ice and Dean, 95.

Him as such, or two, find some other explanation for the power He was demonstrating. They could not deny that Jesus had ability to exorcise demons. All they could do was deny that this was evidence of His Messianic claims. So they blasphemously attributed that power to the Prince of Darkness, saying, "This man casts out demons only by Beelzebul the ruler of the demons" (12:24).

Jesus then went on to show that His ability to "bind the strongman (Satan)" and plunder his kingdom was proof that He was acting by God's power and not Satan's. If, indeed, God was at work, and Jesus had unprecedented power over demons, then Jesus was the Messiah.

The point is hard to miss: "Jesus' encounters with the demons were directly related to His claim to be the Messiah and His offer of the Kingdom."[14] By taking power over Satan and demons, sickness, disease, and even death, Jesus gave a preview of the glorious conditions that will exist during the promised Messianic Kingdom when Satan will be bound and the effects of the curse will be lifted.[15] In spite of His exhibition of power, and in spite of the clear, undeniable demonstration of His Messianic credentials, the nation rejected its Messiah and tragically crucified Him on a Roman cross.[16]

New Testament Usage

There is another indication in Scripture that Jesus' confrontation with the demonic was intended to be unique and not normative. We can look at the frequency with which the New Testament refers to demons and the type of references that are made.

The Greek word for "demon" (*daimonion*) and its related words are used seventy-seven times in the New Testament. The breakdown is as follows:

---

[14] Ibid.

[15] Revelation 20:1-6.

[16] We observe that many of the same signs were done by the Apostles. We will deal with this in more detail in the next chapter where we will see the reason this power was given to the Apostles. As with the Lord, the signs of the Apostles were proof that they spoke and acted on behalf of God.

Four Gospels: 67
Epistles: 7
Revelation: 3

A similar proportion is found when we look at the use of "evil/unclean spirits" which occurs 42 times in the New Testament:

Four Gospels: 23
Acts: 13
Epistles: 3
Revelation: 3

Putting all the references together, we find that "demons/evil spirits/unclean spirits" are mentioned with the following frequency:

Four Gospels: 90
Acts: 13
Epistles: 10
Revelation: 6

We should not miss the fact that Acts and the Gospels are historical books which chronicle the unique Messianic ministry, works, and claims of Jesus Christ and the founding of the church by His personally appointed apostles. Fully eighty-seven percent (103) of the 119 references to demons is contained in this historical section of the New Testament. This is another indication that the encounters of Jesus and the Apostles were unique and not normative.

The epistles (Romans-Jude) are written specifically to churches, pastors, and individual Christians. These epistles address issues that arose in the church and give instruction on how believers are to walk in Christ and conduct themselves in the world and in the church. Yet the epistles *do not* warn believers to look out for demon-possession. They *do not* mention any of the practices promoted by deliverance ministry teachers. They *do not* give any command to exorcise demons. They *do not* contain any instruction on how to exorcise demons, or how to conduct a deliverance session or deliverance ministry.

Instruction on these issues is glaringly absent from the entire New Testament!

Yes, the epistles mention Satan and demons, but only ten times, and most of these are factual statements about their defeat at the cross, or their attempts to deceive and attack believers. By contrast, the Christian's most powerful and dangerous enemy, the flesh, is mentioned fifty times!

Why was there so much demonic activity in the time of Jesus? Does the same thing go on today? I concede that in many cultures around the world, demonic manifestations are much more prevalent than that to which we in the West are exposed. Where worship of demons through idols is the norm, we would expect much more blatant activity than in a culture that is still enjoying the fruit - though quickly fading - of a Christian worldview.

By any standard, the activity of the kingdom of darkness surrounding the ministry of Jesus was exceptional. His arrival in this world and His subsequent Messianic ministry stirred up activity and resistance from Satan that was previously unnoticed. The presence of the Son of God caused the kingdom of darkness to manifest itself in abnormal ways (Mark 1:21-28).

Across the road from my backyard are several unoccupied lots which, without occasional mowing, grow very tall with grass and weeds. On a calm summer evening when I sit in the backyard and look across the grass, I would be led to believe that the tall grass is quiet and void of activity. However, a walk through the grass would reveal something different. The field will come alive with bugs, gnats, grasshoppers, mosquitoes and even garter snakes. What causes the sudden flurry of activity? The presence of a human being walking nearby upsets all the normal activity and reveals what was always going on in the field. The human presence did not create the bug activity. The bugs were there all along, active, living, going about their business. The presence of a human walking through the field stirs up the bug activity.

A similar thing happened during the life and ministry of our Lord. Demons had always been present and active, just as they are today, but the incarnation of Jesus and His real physical presence among men caused the activity of the demons to become noticeable. His very presence caused a stir in the spiritual realm. Suddenly Satan's prisoners were being set free, darkness was dissipated by light, and the blind began to see. God's redemptive plan was about to be culminated and the kingdom of darkness was assaulted by the very King of Light. A spiritual frenzy in the demonic realm ensued. Again, it was a unique time with unique circumstances.

What Are We to Model?

Does this mean that nothing Jesus said or did can serve as a model for us? Certainly not! The apostles pointed to elements of Christ's character and conduct (1 Peter 2:21-25) as things to be followed and imitated. We are enjoined to be conformed to Christ in His character and conduct, but we are never commanded or instructed to imitate His ministry or to mimic those things that relate uniquely to His Messianic Office.

Jesus walked on water, multiplied food, and turned water into wine, but nobody (other than extreme wackos) suggests that we have the authority and/or power to do the same. Further, nobody suggests (again, other than extreme wackos) that these things are to be normative or that we have a responsibility to do the same things.

In fact, if all the power of the Throne of God is ours to use, as Bubeck and Anderson suggest, and we are to model our life after Jesus, then why don't we get any instruction from them on how to turn water to wine or bread to stones, to multiply fish, or to walk on water? Wouldn't Christians who live in depressed and impoverished regions of the world benefit by tapping into their God-ordained authority over all things in order to feed multitudes from just a little food? This authority could keep countless people from starvation. Yet Bubeck and Anderson give us long lists of instructions on how to use this authority to conquer Satan, but not a mention on how to use it for any other purpose. Why does this authority only apply to demons and Satan? Is Jesus not Lord over Creation, nature, the weather, and all physical things? If He is, as evidenced by His exaltation to the right hand of the Father, then do we not share that same power and authority? Why don't Bubeck and Anderson give us

157

some instruction on how to control the weather, multiply bread, and raise the dead?

Obviously, they do not intend for their teaching to be taken to that conclusion, but why not? They have claimed more authority than even they can demonstrate. Their argument proves too much!

Back to "Spot the Flaw"

So what is wrong with the argument I laid out at the beginning? Where did the wheels fall off on the road between "Jesus has all authority" and "I have all authority"?

For starters, as I have already pointed out, there is the *assumed* but unbiblical idea that I am called to imitate *everything* Jesus ever did, even those things unique to His Messianic office and claims.

Second, we should not overlook a very significant difference between Jesus and us, namely, He is God and we are not! Though the argument I offered started with the statement, "Jesus is God," that distinction and identity is quickly forgotten or ignored when trying to argue that I have the same authority as He does. No matter what is true of me spiritually, and no matter what blessings I have received, I am not God incarnate. By virtue of that distinction alone, we are not warranted to presume upon His authority.

Third, it is true that Jesus is seated at the position of power at the right hand of the Father (Ephesians 1:18-20). It is also true that by virtue of my faith in Him, I am *spiritually* seated with Christ in the heavenlies (Ephesians 2:5-6). However, it is not true that this exaltation entitles me to all of the authority and power that He possesses as the divine, exalted Son.

Though the Ephesian passages are quoted as proof of a believer's authority, they have nothing at all to do with spiritual warfare. In fact, that is entirely foreign to the context. Those passages have to do with our acceptance with the Father by virtue of being "in Christ." [17] It is our union with Christ that entitles us to all the blessings listed in Ephesians. We are with Christ and belong to Him. That is the rich truth of those passages. It is a leap to infer that all His

---

[17] Notice the repetition of "in Christ" in the first three chapters of Ephesians.

158

heavenly authority over the physical and spiritual realms is at our disposal.

The flaw was taking one truth and inferring an entire theology of authority over demons from it. Nowhere in Scripture - nowhere - are we told that all believers have authority over Satan and demons. We are told that Christ does. We are told that we belong to Him. That is as far as we are justified in going.

His victory is ours since we are in Him. Therefore, we can resist the devil, steadfast in the faith and standing firm. Our position with Christ entitles us to the confidence to stand in His victory and resist Satan in His strength. It does not entitle us to His authority.

Stand, therefore!

12

What about Exorcisms?

So what about exorcisms? For many today, this is an essential part of effective spiritual warfare. In fact, many ministries and proponents of aggressive spiritual warfare tactics would claim that the exorcism of demons is an indispensable part of waging effective warfare against the kingdom of darkness. The practice of conducting exorcisms is virtually taken for granted in the Christian community. One could almost be labeled a false teacher in some circles for even questioning it.

The popularity of authors Bob Larson and Neil T. Anderson have helped make the practice of exorcisms commonplace in modern evangelicalism.

I have met believers who have claimed at one time to be demon-possessed. One person claimed that he was possessed by demons after he had become a Christian. I have met pastors who have supposedly performed exorcisms as part of ritual deliverance.

A quick perusal of Christian television shows, magazines, and popular books will reveal that most in the Christian community think nothing of promoting the practice of exorcisms or believing that they should be commonplace today. In many circles, people are taught that true spiritual warfare involves exorcising demons out of almost anyone who will stand still long enough for you to lay hands on them.

Matter of Perspective

There is a clear divide between two very different perspectives on spiritual warfare. On the one hand, there are those who view spiritual warfare as a head-to-head encounter with the demonic hordes, by which those demonic hordes are conquered and held at bay through certain prayers, incantations, and tactics. This perspective views spiritual warfare as a battle over territory. Peoples and cities must be claimed, fought for, and taken from the kingdom of darkness. The power and authority of Christ is ours to use for this end.

The second view of spiritual warfare, the one I have advocated, is one in which the battle is primarily over truth. Spiritual warfare is not a battle over territory, but a battle in which ideologies are brought down by the truth of God's Word. People are delivered from the lies of the kingdom of darkness. Though it is true that our enemies are real, we are not engaged in hand-to-hand or head-to-head power encounters with the hosts of darkness. We are called to stand (Ephesians 6:10-17).

Your view of spiritual warfare will play a determinative role in your view of exorcisms. If you believe that spiritual warfare is a series of power encounters that involve direct confrontation of Satan and his demonic powers, then you will likely see exorcisms as an indispensable weapon in your arsenal. If, however, you view spiritual warfare as a battle over truth, and believe that we are called to stand in the truth, walk in the truth, proclaim the truth, and leave the results to God, then you will likely not see exorcisms as something that fits well in that paradigm.

To determine whether or not we are commissioned to perform exorcisms, we need to examine what the New Testament says about them. But first, allow me to offer a bit of historical perspective on the popularity of exorcisms.

Deliverance Ministry in Historical Perspective

According to David Powlison, "Although the practice of exorcism has enjoyed popularity at various times and places in church history, the use of exorcism as a means of accomplishing sanctification - or creating conditions for successful evangelism - is a recent innovation."[1]

---

[1] David Powlison, "Deliverance Ministry In Historical Perspective," *Christian Research Journal* 21. 3 (1998): Article DA086. The information regarding the history of deliverance ministries and theology was gleaned from this article.

The view of spiritual warfare critiqued in this book is of recent origin. It has only been around and developing since the 1960s. Early charismatics were the first to popularize this view of spiritual warfare and its connection to exorcisms. It was pioneered by Pastor Don Basham in his book *Deliver Us from Evil* (1972). His version of demon-deliverance warfare lives on in the ministries of men like Benny Hinn.

A little later, some other well known non-charismatic authors gave credence to the practice of exorcisms in books that did not emphasize spectacular power encounters, but promoted exorcisms as a means of pastoral counseling and sanctification. This approach arose in the circles around Dallas Theological Seminary and Moody Bible Institute. Authors such as Mark Bubeck, Merrill Unger, and C. Fred Dickason became well-known for their "warfare-praying" formulas.

Still later, another variety of exorcism teaching arose, centering around Fuller Theological Seminary and the Vineyard Movement. Authors like John Wimber, C. Peter Wagner, Charles Kraft, John White, and Wayne Grudem offered a perspective that included "signs and wonders" as tools for sanctification, church growth, and Third World missions. Beginning in the 1990s, broadly evangelical authors like Neil T. Anderson and Frank Peretti popularized a theology of demons, spiritual warfare, and exorcisms that is now taken for granted in most evangelical circles.

The determining factor for us in our theology of exorcisms is what the New Testament reveals about them. We must build our theology not on what any particular author says, and certainly not on what I say, but what Scripture reveals. To that we now turn.

The Bible on Exorcisms

The New Testament consistently classifies exorcisms as a "sign" or "wonder." Most people do not think that exorcisms are in any way related to the biblical miracles, but they are. In fact, the relationship is undeniable.

Interestingly, many Christians who would never suggest that we should be performing miracles as the apostles did don't give a second thought to suggesting that we should be performing exorcisms. Exorcisms are included as some of the "signs" done by Jesus and the apostles. If an exorcism is a miracle, and we are not called to perform miracles today, then why would someone think that we should be performing exorcisms today? An exorcism is an example of a biblical miracle.

Those who support the practice of exorcisms are quick to quote the Gospels and the book of Acts to prove their case. As already noted, they believe that the ministry of Jesus and the apostles should serve as a pattern for us to emulate. But let's take a look at what the book of Acts teaches about exorcisms.

1. Exorcisms are classified as "signs and wonders."

There are four passages in the book of Acts that mention exorcisms; Acts 5:12-16; 8:6-7; 16:16-18; and 19:11-12. We will examine each one in turn.

At the hands of the apostles *many signs and wonders* were taking place among the people; (and they were all with one accord in Solomon's portico. But none of the rest dared to associate with them; however, the people held them in high esteem. And all the more believers in the Lord, multitudes of men and women, were constantly added to their number), to such an extent that they even carried the sick out into the streets and laid them on cots and pallets, so that when Peter came by at least his shadow might fall on any one of them. Also the people from the cities in the vicinity of Jerusalem were coming together, bringing people who were sick or *afflicted with unclean spirits, and they were all being healed* (Acts 5:12-16).[2]

The last part of verses 12-14 is a parentheses. Those words which describe the unity of the people and the esteem with which the apostles were viewed interrupt the flow of the sentence which speaks of signs and wonders. If we remove Luke's parenthetical

---

[2] Emphasis mine.

statement, it is easier to see what Luke tells us about signs and wonders.

We are told, "At the hands of the apostles many signs and wonders were taking place among the people." Luke then tells us what these signs and wonders were. There were spectacular healings, such that if the shadow of Peter fell on anyone, he or she was healed. Notice the end of verse 14: Those "who were sick or afflicted with unclean spirits" were brought to the apostles "and they were all being healed."

In that passage, Luke describes two types of miracles. There were physical healings, and there were deliverances from demons. Whether the people were sick or possessed by evil spirits, they were all being healed. Exorcism is described in that passage as a "healing miracle."

The second passage in the book of Acts tells us the same thing. The crowds with one accord were giving attention to what was said by Philip, as they heard and saw the signs which he was performing. For in the case of many who had unclean spirits, they were coming out of them shouting with a loud voice; and many who had been paralyzed and lame were healed (Acts 8:6-7).

The crowds were paying attention to Philip's gospel proclamation because they "heard and saw the signs which he was performing." What kind of "signs" was Philip doing? Again, Luke does not leave us in the dark as to what they were. In the case of those who had "unclean spirits," the spirits were coming out of them. In the cases of those who had been "paralyzed," they were healed. Again, what is an exorcism? It is a sign. It is a miracle. It is classified as a "sign and wonder."

What about the third instance of exorcism in Acts?

It happened that as we were going to the place of prayer, a slave-girl having a spirit of divination met us, who was bringing her masters much profit by fortune-telling. Following after Paul and us, she kept crying out, saying, "These men are bond-servants of the Most High God, who are proclaiming to you the way of salvation." She continued doing this for many days. But Paul was greatly annoyed, and turned and said to the spirit, "I command you in the name of Jesus Christ to come out of her!" And it came out at that very moment (Acts 16:16-18).

You'll notice that this exorcism is not called a "sign" or "wonder." However, it is still an exorcism, and we learn some important things from it.

First, we should note who performed this exorcism: Paul, the apostle. That is significant because, as we will see later, with rare exception, the only ones to perform miracles in the book of Acts were the apostles. Keeping in mind that Luke viewed exorcisms as "miracles," it does not surprise us to see an apostle performing an exorcism. That is what we would expect from men who had miracle-working ability.

Second, Paul obviously did not view exorcisms as necessary for the advancement of the gospel. The text says that this fortune-telling slave girl followed Paul and Silas around for "many days." One wonders why Paul would tolerate this for "many days" before finally exorcising the demon. If we are called to exorcise demons out of anyone and everyone as part of our evangelistic strategy, then this should have been the first thing Paul did when he arrived in Philippi.

Third, notice that the demon "came out at that very moment." It was an instantaneous healing and deliverance. There was no long, protracted "battle" involving detailed incantation-like prayers, [3] sending demons to "the pit," "binding Satan," or naming individual demon principalities. There is nothing said here of renouncing sin, ancestral curses, researching territorial spirits, or a hedge of thorns. Paul spoke the word and it was over, much as we would expect of an exorcism, like a healing, is a miracle.

The fourth passage in the book of Acts is Acts 19:11-12: "God was performing extraordinary miracles by the hands of Paul, so that handkerchiefs or aprons were even carried from his body to the sick,

---

[3] Prayers like those are typical of the writings and ministries of Mark Bubeck, Neil T. Anderson, John Dawson, and Bob Larson.

and the diseases left them and the evil spirits went out." These events took place in Ephesus.

We can observe a few things here which are consistent with the other mentions of exorcisms in Acts. First, we see an apostle mentioned in connection with "extraordinary miracles." Second, Luke does not leave us in the dark as to what these miracles entailed; God used handkerchiefs and aprons carried from Paul to bring healing to the sick. Third, there are two types of miracles mentioned in this passage: the sick were healed as "diseases left them," and "evil spirits went out." Both the healings and the exorcisms are called "extraordinary miracles" wrought by the "hands of Paul," an apostle.

Luke mentions exorcisms four times in the book of Acts. Three of those four times, he calls them miracles, signs, or wonders. Further, we notice that three times they happened at the hands of an apostle, and once by someone commissioned by the apostles and connected to their ministry.

If we learn anything about exorcisms from the book of Acts, it is this: everyone who had power over demons also had power to heal the sick and raise the dead. The same would be said of Jesus. He demonstrated power over demons and He had power to heal the sick and raise the dead. Ironically, many Christians who would never think of claiming the power to heal the sick and raise the dead nevertheless believe they have power over Satan and his demons.

It is also obvious that not everyone performed exorcisms. Not every Christian had this power. If every Christian had this ability then why would Luke call exorcisms "extraordinary miracles"? The only person to perform an exorcism who was not an apostle was Philip, and he was closely associated with apostolic ministry. In fact, we have a well-known account of some who were not apostles who attempted to perform an exorcism: the sons of Sceva (Acts 19:11-20). That did not turn out well.[4]

---

[4] Some might argue that the sons of Sceva were unbelieving Jews and not Christians and therefore what happened to them only serves to show that unbelievers cannot perform exorcisms but does not prove that Christians cannot. That might be true, but Luke seems to be sharing the incident to show that Paul (an apostle) was unique, since God was performing extraordinary miracles by his hands (Acts 19:11). But more to the point, there is no record in

Nor does it seem, from the record of Acts, that exorcisms were commonplace. In the entire time span covered in the book of Acts (thirty years), Luke only mentions exorcisms four times and only records the details of one (Acts 16:12-16). It was hardly central to the spread of the gospel or the ministry of the church at large.

Exorcisms showed that the apostles had God's authority, the same authority as Christ Himself. Christ's work of casting out demons demonstrated His messianic credentials and His deity. The apostles' ability to do the same was evidence that they were Christ's representatives directly commissioned by Him. We only see legitimate exorcisms happening at the hands of Jesus, His apostles, and, in *one instance*, someone directly commissioned by the apostles.

2. The New Testament teaches that the ability to perform "signs and wonders" was given to the apostles for the purpose of authenticating apostolic ministry and authority.

Consider the following Scriptures:

Acts 2:43: "Everyone kept feeling a sense of awe; and many *wonders and signs* were taking place *through the apostles*."

Acts 5:12: "At the *hands of the apostles* many *signs and wonders* were taking place among the people; and they were all with one accord in Solomon's portico."

Acts 14:3: "Therefore they spent a long time there speaking boldly with reliance upon the Lord, who was testifying to the word of His grace, granting that *signs and wonders* be done by *their hands*." (The "they" spoken of refers to Paul and Barnabas in 13:50.)

Acts 15:12: "All the people kept silent, and they were listening to Barnabas and *Paul* as they were relating what *signs and wonders* God had done through them among the Gentiles."

Acts 19:11: "God was performing *extraordinary miracles* by the *hands of Paul.* "

Acts of an average Christian performing an exorcism. I believe that is because Christians understood that was not their prerogative any more than other miraculous abilities were.

2 Corinthians 12:12: "The *signs* of a true *apostle* were performed among you with all perseverance, by *signs* and *wonders* and *miracles*."

Hebrews 2:3-4: "How will we escape if we neglect so great a salvation? After it was at the first spoken through the Lord, it was *confirmed* to us by *those who heard*, God also testifying with *them*, both by *signs* and *wonders* and by various *miracles* and by gifts of the Holy Spirit according to His own will." (Those who heard the Lord did the signs. This is a reference to the apostles.)[5]

The signs that the apostles performed serve the same purpose as the signs that Jesus performed. They serve as an authentication of their ministry. Their ability to perform the same kinds of signs that Jesus did demonstrated that they were truly sent and commissioned by Him (2 Corinthians 12:12); they were true apostles. As the author to the Hebrews says, God confirmed their word by "testifying with them, both by signs and wonders and by various miracles."

There are only three exceptions to this: Stephen (Acts 6:8), Philip (Acts 8:6-7), and Barnabas (Acts 14:3). In each of these three cases, the persons performing the miracles were closely associated with the apostles and apostolic ministries.

We can conclude from the passages we have examined that the New Testament teaches that exorcisms are miracles, and miracles were done by apostles or those very closely associated with the apostles.

Absence of Instruction

There are *no* instructions in the epistles of the New Testament on the subject of exorcisms. The silence of the rest of the New Testament is deafening. We do not find either the apostles or Jesus giving any instructions to the church for conducting exorcisms.

We are never commanded to exorcise demons. We are never instructed on how to exorcise demons. We do not even get the sense from the New Testament that we are expected to exorcise demons. If exorcisms are to be commonplace today, then it is unthinkable that the Lord would remain silent and leave us no instruction on how to

---

[5] Emphasis added.

engage such a dangerous, powerful, and deceptive enemy in that fashion.

You can read the New Testament from Romans to Revelation and you will not find one word of instruction or command regarding exorcising demons. The best way to account for this obvious silence is the fact that exorcisms are miracles performed by Jesus and the apostles to authenticate their message and ministry, and that exorcisms were never intended to continue beyond the apostolic era.

If you want instruction on conducting exorcisms, you cannot turn to the New Testament. Instead, you are forced to turn to the writings of modern-day deliverance ministry "experts" for their detailed directions. They are quick to suggest methodologies, prayers, incantations, and renunciations.

Mark Bubeck offers "some cautions and warnings lest some might be prone to rush into bold encounter [sic] carelessly."[6] What follows in his book are three full pages of helpful suggestions, tips, and tricks for conducting exorcisms. Where Scripture is silent, Bubeck rushes in with a list of do's and don't's. Among the many spiritual qualifications for an exorcism that Bubeck offers we find the following:

- One should be committed to the Lordship of Christ.
- One needs to practice Scripture memorization.
- Avoid working with someone not committed and surrendered to the Lordship of Christ.[7]

Bubeck offers a list of things you should not do during an exorcism, including the following:

- Don't seek information or allow any wicked spirit to volunteer information you do not seek.
- Don't believe what a wicked spirit says unless you test it.
- Don't assume that one victory is the end of the warfare.

---

[6] Mark Bubeck, *The Adversary* (Chicago: Moody Press, 1975), 122.
[7] Ibid., 122-123.

- Don't rely upon bold confrontation as the main way to victory over the enemy.[8]

No list would be complete without "the dos," and Bubeck is never slow to fill in what Scripture lacks.

- Do daily put on the whole armor of God and claim your union with Christ and walk in the fullness of the Holy Spirit.
- Do take back all ground you may have given Satan by careless willful sins of the flesh.
- Do bind all powers of darkness working under any wicked spirit to him, commanding them all to leave when he does.
- Do force the wicked spirit to admit that because you are seated with Christ far above all principalities and powers that you have full authority over them.
- Do force them to admit that when you command them to leave, they have to go where Christ sends them.
- Do demand that if the wicked power has divided into several parts, that he become a whole spirit.
- Do be prepared for the wicked power to try to hurt the person you're working with in some manner.[9]

It is obvious that these instructions are not found anywhere in Scripture. If these are essential for exorcisms, and if the Lord neglected to give us these instructions, then He has truly done us a disservice. It would lead one to conclude that the Word of God is not sufficient. Are we to believe that the church had to wait for Mark Bubeck and Neil Anderson to arrive on the scene to give us this essential information about conducting exorcisms? Where would we be without these men to fill in where Scripture lacks?

---

[8] Ibid., 124.
[9] Ibid., 124-125.

But What About...

If our understanding of Scripture is correct, and I believe it is, then there is an obvious contradiction between what Scripture teaches and what some have claimed to experience or witness. Someone is sure to object by citing an experience either personal or anecdotal. I too know people who have supposedly done exorcisms, witnessed them, or had demons exorcised from them. What do we make of these experiences?

As previously stated, we don't build our theology on our experiences, regardless of how real and convincing they may be. We build our thinking from Scripture and then ask, "How do I understand what I have experienced in light of Scripture?"

If the Bible says that genuine exorcisms are miracles, and if the Bible says the miracles were performed by Jesus and the apostles, and if the apostles are no longer living, and if the Bible does not command us or give us instructions on exorcising demons, then there is only one conclusion to draw: the so-called exorcisms of today are not the genuine article.

Might I suggest that it is at least theoretically possible that the father of lies, the great deceiver, the angel of light, may be deceiving people into thinking that they can control him? Is it possible that Satan is leading people, well-intentioned as they are, into practices which are utterly useless? Is it possible that he might want people to focus on activities that make no difference and distract God's people from the real issues, namely the proclamation and defense of the gospel? I certainly think that that is a viable explanation.

Christians today do not have the power to cast out demons any more than they have the power to turn water into wine or raise the dead. We can't perform signs and wonders. Modern exorcisms are nothing more than demonic deceptions craftily designed to get Christians sidetracked from the real war, which is a truth war.

The experiences of modern-day exorcisms are created by something other than the power of God. Pagan religions also have exorcisms. Hindu gurus perform exorcisms and people are apparently delivered from demons by them. These are clearly not done by the power of God. Jesus said that some would be able to

172

perform exorcisms who would not even be saved (Matthew 7:21-23)! How do we account for those exorcisms? Are they the real McCoy? Or is Satan deceiving those in pagan religions and H:ndu cults? If Satan is deceiving those in pagan religions and Hindu cults by fabricating false exorcisms, what makes us think he cannot or would not do the same to Christians?

What Is Our Approach?

Do I believe that people today can be demon-possessed? I most certainly do. I do not believe that Christians can be demon-possessed, but I do believe that it is possible for nonbelievers to be controlled and possessed by demons. How then should we deal with demon-possessed unbelievers? The same way we deal with non-demon-possessed unbelievers - share the gospel.[10]

What does a demon-possessed person need? Does he need an exorcism or a power encounter? What is it the Scripture says delivers us from the kingdom of darkness and translates us to the kingdom of light? What is it that sets us free from sin, Satan, and self? What is the power of God unto salvation? It is the gospel (Rom. 1:16). In order to be set free from Satan, the unbeliever needs the glorious light of the gospel of Christ.

Advocates of deliverance ministries would argue that a demon-possessed person first needs to be exorcised of his demon(s) before the gospel can be received by him. They teach that if we don't exorcise the demons first, the demon will prevent him from receiving Christ.

This view presumes the demon-possessed person is worse off than the average unregenerate garden-variety pagan. Is something more than the gospel necessary to deliver someone from the kingdom of darkness to light? Is the gospel insufficient to effect this transformation? Is the gospel message itself not powerful enough to bring freedom from Satan? The whole notion that something *more* than gospel proclamation is necessary for the salvation of a demon-possessed sinner, is an affront to the power of the gospel message,

---

[10] I would doubt that most of us run across demon-possessed people on a daily basis.

and I don't buy it. Where in the Bible do we read that a demon-possessed person is less likely to trust Christ than a non-demon-possessed person? Isn't the non-demon-possessed person just as much a "child of wrath," "dead in sin," and "hostile to God" unbeliever as a demon-possessed person is?

A demon-possessed person does not need a power encounter. They need a truth encounter. They don't need an exorcism, they need the gospel. When that person trusts Christ for salvation, they will be set free entirely from sin, demons, and Satan. The gospel proclaimed is powerful enough to deliver an unbeliever from darkness. It does not need our carnal methods accompanied by the fanciful advice of deliverance ministry "experts."

Thomas Ice and Robert Dean rightly state,

The norm for dealing with demon-possessed unbelievers has become the preaching of the gospel. . . . Any believer can deliver another person from demons by leading him to Christ. The Scriptures do not require a second-step deliverance for a believer in order that he may be freed from the demonic; Christ sweeps the house clean at the moment of salvation.[11]

Are Exorcisms for Today?

Exorcisms are miracles. They were miracles done by Jesus and the apostles. We are not commanded to do exorcisms. We are not instructed on how to do exorcisms. The New Testament does not expect us to do exorcisms. In view of these truths, we have to conclude that the answer is no. Exorcisms are not necessary for the spread of the gospel, the salvation of the sinner, or the sanctification of the saints.

Stand firm in the truth.

---

[11] Thomas Ice and Robert Dean, *Overrun By Demons: The Church's New Preoccupation With The Demonic* (Eugene: Harvest House Publishers, 1990), 128.

13

Spiritual Warfare and Sanctification

Few things are more obvious to a new believer than the reality of persistent remaining sin. The regenerating work of the Holy Spirit and His indwelling bring an awareness of sin that the unregenerate person is incapable of knowing. Suddenly, a new believer sees sins in his life and feels compelled to battle against them. Since Scripture teaches that the unredeemed flesh persists with us until death (Romans 7-8), this constant war against sin can be very discouraging and perplexing to a new Christian.

This experience results not from an increase in the number of temptations or an increase in sinful desires. Rather, we become more aware of sin as a result of being indwelt by the Holy Spirit. Regeneration brings a new principle of life and righteousness into our lives that was absent prior to conversion. Suddenly we begin to progress in sanctification and find that we have a desire for righteousness which wars against the desires of the flesh.

The converted drunkard suddenly finds that sobriety is not so easy. The man whose mind has been flooded for years with pornography finds that the battle does not go away overnight. The inveterate adulteress finds that controlling her habitually flirtatious ways is suddenly more difficult than she first imagined. The foulmouthed person is suddenly aware that the tongue is a deadly evil and controlling his speech takes constant vigilance and discipline. So it goes with every sin, every habit, and every temptation.

Being untrained in righteousness (Romans 6:15-23) the new Christian can begin to feel as if victory over sin and progression in holiness is a lost cause. Discouragement can set in and before long he

175

or she starts to desire a "quick fix," a remedy, a system or program which promises immediate victory and instant results. The predominant view of spiritual warfare which I have been examining in this book offers just such a false remedy.

Spiritual Warfare to the Rescue

If you're familiar with the methods of spiritual warfare advocated by the popular authors I have mentioned, then you are also likely familiar with the way in which their view of the spirit world and spiritual warfare is applied to the progressive sanctification of a believer. All of the practices which have proved to be unbiblical are inevitably used in the battle against sin. The result can be nothing short of disastrous. Waging spiritual warfare with the wrong methodology is certain to result in distraction and defeat. Likewise, pursuing sanctification through the wrong means or battling sin with the wrong weapons cannot bring about the victory we desire.

The modern teaching on spiritual warfare treats the spiritual battle as a war for territory. The Bible describes true spiritual warfare as a war for truth. Those two different views lead to two radically different methodologies of spiritual warfare and two different approaches to progressive sanctification.

The "territory view" of spiritual warfare teaches that sin in the life of a believer is caused by demonic strongholds, oppression, curses, territorial spirits, or even demon possession. The answers they propose to the problems include the very things I have already critiqued and shown to be either unbiblical or extra-biblical. If someone misdiagnoses a disease, they will also misdiagnose the cure.

Getting Sin and Satan Wrong

"The Devil made me do it" is not just a well-known Flip Wilson line, but it is also a staple of modern evangelical spiritual warfare theology. Satan gets far more credit for creating sin in the life of a believer than he deserves. He not only gets credit for causing sin, but according to some, he is also the primary cause of disease in the lives of God's people.

176

Famed (and shamed) televangelist Robert Tilton was quite fond of raging at the demonic forces that he believed to be tormenting and attacking his television audience. I mentioned this tirade in an earlier chapter. Read this again, only this time notice who gets the credit for causing various sins and sicknesses. On one episode of his *Success-N-Life* program, he ranted,

Satan, you demonic spirits of AIDS, and AIDS virus - I bind you! You demon-spirits of cancer, arthritis, infection, migraine headaches, pain - come out of that body! Come out of that child! Come out of that man. . . . Satan, I bind you! You foul demon-spirits of sickness and disease. Infirmities in the inner ear and the lungs and the back. You demon spirits of arthritis, sickness, and disease. You tormenting, infirm spirits in the stomach. Satan, I bind you! You nicotine spirits - I bind you! In the name of Jesus![1]

Tilton's bizarre way of linking a smoking addiction to the work of "nicotine spirits" kinda makes you wonder what "nicotine spirits" did before the invention of cigarettes!

Not only is Satan given credit for causing sickness and disease in the life of a believer, but often he receives the credit for causing us to sin. It is not uncommon for those in deliverance ministries to go so far as to attribute gluttony, hatred, jealousy, envy, gossip, murder, homosexuality, pride, drunkenness, and even suicide to demons. A quick online search will turn up dozens of "deliverance ministry" websites dedicated to dealing with the demons which are supposedly attached to all these sins and many more.

Mark Bubeck, for instance, claims that a demon once named himself as "Suicide."[2] During a confrontation with demonic powers which Bubeck supposedly had for the sake of delivering his daughter from demonic oppression (or possession),[3] he commanded demons

---

1. Robert Tilton, *Success-N-Life* program (ca. 1991), video on file at Christian Research Institute. This was quoted by Hank Hanegraaff, *Christianity in Crisis* (Eugene: Harvest House Publishers, 1993), 257.

2 Mark I. Bubeck, *The Adversary* (Chicago: Moody Press, 1975),91-92.

3 This encounter was detailed in Chapter 9.

177

"in the name of the Lord Jesus Christ," to state their names. Bubeck reports,

> We were able to get the names of a hierarchy that was set on destroying Judy, and through her problems would be able to attack my ministry. Some of the names given were identical to the symptoms described.[4] Fear was the head of the hierarchy, under him were such workers as Nausea, Colon, Destroyer, and Deceiver.[5]

This is typical of the approach of those who believe that a demon is behind every sin or symptom.

Bubeck does not glean any of this insight from Scripture, since Scripture never gives these names, or any like them, for demons. The only way Bubeck could get this information is by conversing with demons - a patently unbiblical approach, and one fraught with error. Why should we believe that demons are speaking the truth about their names or their involvement? Further, why should I believe that such a practice is even necessary? Why should I even buy his presupposition that the information provided in Scripture is insufficient, and then seek the necessary information from demons? Scripture does not speak of demons named Suicide, Lust, Greed, Envy or Nicotine. This is all mystical, experience-based, superstitious nonsense!

Bubeck, like White, Anderson, and others, views sin in the life of a believer as the work of demons. Here is how the thinking goes: Lust must be caused by a demon (probably named Lust) who attacks me, distracts me, and puts thoughts in my head. He must have a horde of helpers, all part of a hierarchy, whose names are probably Sensuality, Passion, Distraction, Lewdness, and Hormone. In all likelihood, one of these demons gained a foothold in my family

---

[4] His daughter was experiencing nausea and distress.

[5] Bubeck, 121. Remember that this is the same man who, when giving his list of "dos and don'ts" for exorcisms, tells his reader, "Don't believe what a wicked spirit says unless you test it." Yet here Bubeck believes this testimony that he received from wicked spirits without a word about testing it. What makes him think that these are the actual names of these demons? He just takes them at their word. Perhaps he thinks that since their testimony seemed to jive with his experience, then it was true. If that is the case, then this demonstrates the height of his folly - testing the word of a demon by his own subjective experience.

through my father's repeated sin of adultery. That demon is probably named Adultery (I know, the names can be very confusing, but try and keep up!). Consequently, the devil now has a "foothold" in my life and my home. Since the sins of the fathers are passed down through multiple generations, it is a guarantee that I, and my sons, and my sons' sons struggle with the same sins. These demons and their influence have been entrenched in my life. Thus there is a spiritual curse upon my family, a demonic stronghold in my life, and demon activity that must be purged.

What must be done, according to modern deliverance ministry teaching? These spiritual forces must be directly confronted and dealt with.

The cure would go something like this: these sins and activities of my father and grandfather would need to be researched, identified, and confessed to God. I would need to "plead the blood of Jesus" over these sins and renounce verbally to the spirit world my repudiation of the sins (and don't forget the stock formula prayers for just such occasions). One can't be too thorough when trying to break satanic or generational curses, so one needs to be careful to name every sin which might have given this foothold to the devil.

Next, a direct confrontation with the spirits involved, who are conveniently named Lust, Adultery, Passion, Hormone, etc. is necessary. Demanding, in the name of Jesus, of course, that each spirit name himself, and identify the demon powers above and below him in the hierarchy, will help to inform my formulaic prayers against the spirit beings. This is important, since each spirit needs to be bound by name. Prayers such as, "I bind you, you evil spirit of Lust, in the name of Jesus and by His blood. I send you to the pit of hell, or wherever the Lord Jesus would send you," would be employed. And of course, we can't forget the all-important verbal rebuke that must be thrown toward Satan and his demons every so often. Something like, "I rebuke you, Satan, in the name of Jesus! Flee from me!" We might find it necessary to remind Satan that we are children of God, and that we have authority over him to whip him, bind him, and send him to the pit—just in case he might have forgotten.

179

Leading my children (and grandchildren if applicable) in the same process of renunciation and binding is essential if they are to experience any freedom. Next, I would need to pray a hedge of thorns around my belongings, my house, my workplace, my relatives, my spouse, my children, my dog, my favorite football team, and anything else which I might want to protect from Satan's influence.

What a yoke of burden we are saddled with by such false teachings! If that does not leave a person exhausted, depressed, and confused, I don't know what would! If you think the battle is over, if you think the victory is won, you are wrong. Every time that temptation presents itself, you will need to go through the entire laborious process all over again! After all, you can't bind Satan too many times! I can't tell you how many times I heard Satan and his demons bound during Bible college prayer meetings.

This is the taxing, laborious, and misguided method of personal sanctification promoted by those who blame every sin on demons.

If that is not enough, keep in mind that this is the process that needs to be repeated for every sin in your life! Gossip, lying, laziness, fear, pride, slander, drunkenness, lust, greed, covetousness, jealousy, strife, backbiting, anger, doubt, and a host of others, can all be dealt with the same way - at least according to the teachings of modern-day deliverance ministry "experts."

What's Wrong with this Picture?

Scripture does not describe sin as the result of possession, oppression, or curses in the life of a believer. Those things which modern deliverance ministry "experts" attribute to *demons*, are the works of the *flesh*. Galatians 5 says that the "deeds of the flesh are evident, which are: immoralities, impurity, sensuality, idolatry, sorcery, enmities, strife, jealousy, outbursts of anger, disputes, dissensions, factions, envying, drunkenness, carousing, and things like these. . ." (Galatians 5:19-21).

Attributing these deeds to the activity of demons when Scripture attributes them to the flesh is to misdiagnose the problem. If the problem is misdiagnosed, the proper solution will not be

180

appropriated. Deliverance ministry "experts" attempt to deal with these sins through mantra-like prayers, power encounters, renouncing curses, binding Satan, and/or exorcisms. These are the very practices that we have seen to be completely unbiblical.

As we saw in Chapters 3 and 4, the Christian is involved in a three-front war. We battle against the world, the flesh, and the devil. Any view of spiritual warfare which does not take into account all three enemies is going to fail to offer an approach which can adequately meet all three enemies. In the scenario I have presented, the role of the flesh in the life of the believer and his battle against sin is entirely ignored. This is because Satan gets the blame for the works of the flesh.

If your theology of spiritual warfare fails to properly account for the cause of the problem, then it will also fail to provide a proper solution. Attributing to Satan and his demons the works which Scripture clearly attributes to the flesh, results in treating the wrong problem with the wrong solution.

The misguided emphasis of modern deliverance ministries ends up leading people to shift responsibility for their sin from themselves to Satan.

> Rather than accepting the responsibility for our own sin, we prefer to shift the responsibility to someone or something else. Rather than choosing the biblical solution to confessing and putting to death the deeds of the flesh, we seek to solve the problem by "binding demons" or practicing "exorcisms." Interestingly, passing the buck has been a convenient way of avoiding personal responsibility for sin ever since Adam and Eve.[6]

Neither Satan nor the world can cause us to sin. These things can lure us, tempt us, and distract us, but they cannot make us sin. The source of my sin is not Satan, but my own lust. "But each one is tempted when he is carried away and enticed by his own lust. Then

---

[6] Thomas Ice and Robert Dean Jr., *Overrun By Demons: The Church's New Preoccupation With The Demonic* (Eugene: Harvest House Publishers, 1990), 85.

when lust has conceived, it gives birth to sin; and when sin is accomplished, it brings forth death" (James 1:14-15).

Our problem is not that we have demons possessing us, attacking us, or oppressing us. We have an enemy on the inside–the flesh. As a good friend from Bible college used to say, "Satan doesn't have to expend any effort to tempt me to sin - my flesh is plenty capable of that!"

The Biblical Solution[7]

The Bible does not leave us in the dark when it comes to fighting the war against sin. It not only commands us to pursue holiness (Hebrews 12:14), but instructs us and equips us with all the tools necessary for growth in sanctification.

First, we have to come to grips with the cause of our sin. We cannot shift responsibility for sin from ourselves to Satan. We must own up to the fact that we are sinners, and though we are justified, saved, forgiven, and indwelt by the Spirit of God, we still dwell in unredeemed bodies of sin, fraught with weakness and corruption.

Second, we can be encouraged to know that our sanctification is not entirely the result of our own efforts and abilities. The Holy Spirit is working to take those whom the Father has predestined, called, and justified, and conform them to the image of His Son (Romans 8:28-30). "But we all, with unveiled face, beholding as in a mirror the glory of the Lord, are being transformed into the same image from glory to glory, just as from the Lord, the Spirit" (2 Corinthians 3:18). It is "God who is at work in you, both to will and to work for His good pleasure" (Philippians 2:13).

This does not mean that we have no role or no work in the fight against sin. We are to "work out our own salvation with fear and trembling" (Philippians 2:12), pursue sanctification (Hebrews 12:14),

---

[7] The means by which a believer pursues sanctification, mortifies the flesh, and grows in holiness is a subject worthy of its own book. What follows here is a brief presentation of this issue. For further study I would recommend starting with *Respectable Sins* and *Pursuit of Holiness*, both by Jerry Bridges, and *Christ Formed In* You by Brian G. Hedges. Among older books written by puritans, I would recommend *The Mortification Of Sin* by John Owen, *The Doctrine of Repentance* by Thomas Watson, *Overcoming Sin and Temptation* by John Owen, and *Holiness* by J.C. Ryle.

and discipline ourselves for the purpose of godliness (1 Timothy 4:7). We are commanded to mortify the flesh and put it off its deeds (Colossians 3:1-11). We must also "put on the new man" and his deeds which are created in Christ Jesus (Ephesians 4:17-32). Our work towards sanctification does not crowd out or preclude God's work in us. The fact that God is at work in us does not mean that we have no part in it. This is the paradox of the doctrine of sanctification. I work, yet not I, but the grace of God at work in me.

The Bible consistently describes my sanctification as a work which God does and a work which I do. Consider the following brief list of examples:

In 2 Peter 1:3-5 it is God who has "granted to us His precious and magnificent promises, so that by them you may become partakers of the divine nature, having escaped the corruption that is in the world by lust." That is the work of God. It is by His work and His provision that we have escaped the corruption that is in the world by lust. Yet the very next verse says that we are to "apply all diligence," and in your faith supply moral excellence, knowledge, self-control, perseverance, godliness, brotherly kindness, and love (vv. 5-9). Peter then concludes his thoughts by encouraging us to "be all the more diligent to make certain about His calling in choosing you" (v. 10). It doesn't sound like Peter saw any conflict at all between our work toward sanctification and God's work in us.

James saw no contradiction between submitting to God and the active work of resisting the devil (James 4:7).

Paul said, "I have been crucified with Christ and it is no longer I who live, but Christ lives in me; and the life which I now live in the flesh I live by faith in the Son of God who loved me and gave Himself for me" (Galatians 2:20). Who was it that was responsible for living Paul's Christian life? It was true that he no longer lived - it was *Christ living* in him. Yet it was also true that *he lived* a life in the flesh by faith in the Son of God.

In Colossians 1:28-29, Paul mentions both his work and God's work in him. "We proclaim Him, admonishing every man and teaching every man with all wisdom, so that we may present every man complete in Christ. For this purpose also I labor, striving

183

according to His power, which mightily works within me." It was Paul who worked. It was Paul who labored. It was Paul who did the striving. But it was according to God's power which was at work in him.

In one of my favorite passages, 1 Corinthians 15:10, Paul says, "But by the grace of God I am what I am, and His grace toward me did not prove vain; but I labored even more than all of them, yet not I, but the grace of God within me." Who was it that made Paul what he was? He labored more than all the other apostles, yet it was not Paul, but the grace of God within Paul.

You might be tempted to ask, "Paul, would you please make up your mind? Who's responsible for your sanctification? Who is it that does the work of ministry? Who is it that lives your Christian life? You or God?" The answer to that question is, "Both."

Third, regeneration frees us to obey God and His word. The war against sin involves effort on the part of the Christian to fight against the temptations and desires, the lusts of the flesh. Those do not disappear at the moment of salvation, but neither do they hold us in bondage any longer. "Though you were slaves of sin, you became obedient from the heart to that form of teaching to which you are committed, and having been freed from sin, he became slaves of righteousness" (Romans 6:17-18).

Now, rather than living in subjection to the lusts of the flesh and the dictates of our unredeemed sinful nature, we can live in obedience to God and His Word.

I am speaking in human terms because of the weakness of your flesh. For just as you presented your members as slaves to impurity and to lawlessness, resulting in further lawlessness, so now present your members as slaves to righteousness, resulting in sanctification (Romans 6:19).

At one time we gave ourselves, our bodies, our minds, our time, and our efforts to sin. Now that we have been set free from sin, we are to offer ourselves, our bodies, our minds, our time, and our efforts to righteousness. We are to yield the members of our body to the dictates and commands of righteousness just as we once obeyed sin and its lusts. The result of such obedience to righteousness is sanctification- growth in holiness.

Victory over sin and temptation is as simple as refusing to obey sin and instead yielding our obedience to righteousness. By the grace of God, by the work of the Holy Spirit in us, we work to train ourselves to obey our new Master. Relying on the power of the Holy Spirit, we labor and strive, discipline ourselves for godliness, and yield to obedience. We are able to do this because

We have been buried with Him through baptism into death, so that as Christ was raised from the dead to the glory of the Father, so we too might walk in newness of life. For if we have become united with Him in the likeness of His death, certainly we shall also be in the likeness of His resurrection, knowing this, that our old self was crucified with Him, in order that our body of sin might be done away with, so that we would no longer be slaves to sin; for he who has died is freed from sin (Romans 6:4-7).

Of course we will always be aware of indwelling sin and cry out, "Wretched man that I am! Who will set me free from the body of this death?" (Romans 7:24). Like Paul, we will take comfort in the fact that the Holy Spirit who dwells in us is at work to conform us to the image of God's Son (Romans 8).

Scripture uses a lot of different language to describe our obedience. We are to "discipline ourselves for the purpose of godliness" (1 Timothy 4:7). Scripture says we are to "put to death the deeds of the flesh" (Romans 8:13), "lay aside the old self," and, "put on the new self" (Ephesians 4:22-24), and to "consider the members of your earthly body as dead to immorality, impurity, passion, evil desire, and greed, which amounts to idolatry" (Colossians 3:5). We are to "put aside" the sins of the flesh and "put on the new self who is being renewed to a true knowledge" (Colossians 3:9-10).

Fourth, we need to be diligent to give ourselves to those things which will strengthen us for this battle. We cannot neglect the means of grace that God has given to His people by which we are strengthened, equipped, and aided in our sanctification. The Holy Spirit does not neglect the means, and neither should we.

We should not neglect the gathering of ourselves to corporate worship (Hebrews 10:25), submitting to our leaders (Hebrews 13:17), offering up sacrifices of praise and thanksgiving (Hebrews 13:15), hiding God's Word in our hearts (Psalm 119:9-16), being filled with the Word of God (Colossians 3:16), observing the ordinances of baptism and the Lord's Supper, and submitting to the regular preaching of the Word. All of these, and many more, are the means which God has ordained through which the Holy Spirit conforms us to the image of Christ.

New Affections

No discussion of our growth in holiness would be complete without mentioning the power of a "new affection." Ultimately, victory over temptation and sin is possible only when my affections and desire for sin and self have been replaced by a higher and more compelling affection.

It is only when Christ is precious to us, and more precious than our lusts, our sins, or the perceived benefits of sin, that we will truly flee sin and pursue Christ. This is what theologian Thomas Chalmers referred to as "the expulsive power of a new affection." The new affections which belong to our new nature, begin to push out our old affections: our love for sin and self. A hunger and love for Christ replaces a hunger and love for sin. Pray that God will give you that affection.

We can have no true hope for victory over sin if we harbor in our hearts a love for it. When we love Christ more than sin, it will lose its allure. All our efforts at cultivating a relationship with God should have as their goal satisfaction in the person and the glory of Christ. May God grant that we seek and find our satisfaction in Him.

Part 4:
Examining a Biblical Passage

14

The Posture of a Soldier

You might think that a book on spiritual warfare would *begin* with a study of Ephesians 6, rather than *end* with it. Yet here we are in the last three chapters and we are finally getting around to what is considered the sine qua non of the Bible's teaching on spiritual warfare: the Armor of God. Our study of Ephesians 6 will offer some positive instruction on the subject and summarize what we have covered so far.

As we have discovered, the subject of spiritual warfare has been colored and clouded by all types of gnostic and mystic teachings, abuses of Scripture, and unbiblical practices. If we had jumped right into the "Armor of God" in Ephesians 6, our understanding of the passage would have been polluted by all the unbiblical presuppositions and practices which have become part and parcel of the modern spiritual warfare movement.

Now that we have laid the foundation for our study and affirmed that the Bible is sufficient for the battle in which we are engaged (Chapter 1), and have come to realize that spiritual warfare is a battle for truth and not territory (Chapter 2), and have disabused ourselves of all the extra-biblical and unbiblical practices which clutter the Christian landscape (Chapters 4-13), we can now tackle the teaching of Ephesians 6. We will find that this passage offers clear and concise wisdom concerning the battle in which we are engaged.

Setting the Context for the Armor of God

All too often, Ephesians 6 is treated in isolation from its entire context. If you have been a Christian for any length of time, you may be more familiar with Ephesians 6 than you are with anything else in the book of Ephesians. It is not uncommon to find a series of messages on the subject of spiritual warfare that offers a treatment of

Ephesians 6 without any consistent exposition of the five-and-a-half chapters which preceded it. It makes you wonder if some folks are even aware that Ephesians has five other chapters!

We don't want to make that mistake. I'm convinced that a proper understanding of the Armor of God requires an understanding of the first five-and-a-half chapters of Ephesians. During this chapter and the following, we will be making reference repeatedly to the truths taught in those other five chapters. Let's begin by setting up that context.

When reading or studying Ephesians, we would arrive at Chapter 6, and at first glance the passage seems a little out of place. If you trace the argument and flow of the first five chapters, then the last thing you might expect at the close of the book is a treatise on spiritual warfare.

The first three chapters of Ephesians treat some of the loftiest doctrine that the mind of man could ever approach: election, predestination, adoption, redemption, the glory of God, the sealing of the Spirit, our eternal inheritance, the sovereign will of God, total depravity, justification, and the peace which has been wrought by the death of Christ. The first three chapters cover nearly all of the doctrines of salvation. Paul describes the comprehensive results of God's actions and sovereign work of redeeming sinners.

Paul does not leave those doctrines as mere theoretical propositions but, in the second half of the book, fleshes out the implications of that profound theology as he encourages us to "walk in a manner worthy of the calling with which you have been called" (Ephesians 4:1). He then goes on to address such lofty themes as walking in humility (4:1-6), walking in unity (4:7-16), walking in newness of life (4:17-32), walking in light (5:1-17), and walking in mutual submission (5:18-6:9). Then, it seems, we are suddenly brought into the nitty-gritty, bloody, grimy metaphor of war and talk of demons (6:10-17). However, what appears at first glance to be out of place, ends up being a perfect summary for what Paul has been teaching for the entire book.

Paul is essentially saying, "Now, in the face of tremendous spiritual opposition, put on everything you have been given. Clothe yourself with it. Stand." Since 4:1, Paul has been telling us to appropriate by faith all that has been provided by God's gracious gift of salvation. Chapters 1-3 tell us what it means for us to be "in Christ." Chapters 4-6 tell us what it means to have Christ in us.

We should expect that if we commit ourselves to live out our faith, that we will experience opposition and even persecution (2 Timothy 3:12). Anyone who commits himself to walk in humility rather than pride, in unity rather than division, in love rather than lust, light rather than darkness, wisdom rather than foolishness, the Spirit of God rather than drunkenness, and mutual submission rather than selfishness, is bound to face an enemy that will seek his destruction. That enemy is going to oppose us. He is going to do his best to trick us into pride, selfishness, bitterness, speaking evil, unforgiveness, deeds of darkness, foolishness - the very things from which we have been delivered. The cold reality is that Satan seeks to oppose any believer who truly tries to "walk in the manner worthy of the calling with which he has been called" (Ephesians 4:1).

You will face an enemy, and it is not going to be a cakewalk. It is going to be a fight. The passage before us explains how we are to stand in the salvation we have been given. This passage demonstrates the adequacy of our salvation to shield us against even the devil himself.

Finally, be strong in the Lord and in the strength of His might. Put on the full armor of God, so that you will be able to stand firm against the schemes of the devil. For our struggle is not against flesh and blood, but against the rulers, against the powers, against the world forces of this darkness, against the spiritual forces of wickedness in the heavenly places. Therefore, take up the full armor of God, so that you will be able to resist in the evil day, and having done everything, to stand firm. Stand firm therefore, having girded your loins with truth, and having put on the breastplate of righteousness, and having shod your feet with the preparation of the gospel of peace; in addition to all, taking up the shield of faith with which you will be able to extinguish all the flaming arrows of the evil one. And

191

take the helmet of salvation, and the sword of the Spirit, which is the word of God (Ephesians 6:10-17).

In this chapter we will take a look at what Paul says about the battle in which we are engaged. We will save the individual pieces of the armor and their significance for the next chapter. In the opening verses of the above passage, we see three things we need to know about our struggle: our adequacy is in our Sovereign, our adversary is Satan, and our approach is to stand.

Our Adequacy Is in Our Sovereign

"Finally, be strong in the Lord and in the strength of His might. Put on the full armor of God, so that you will be able to stand firm against the schemes of the devil" (Ephesians 6:10).

Paul begins by directing our attention to the strength we find in the Lord. By His grace and through His enablement God has provided two things.

First, He has provided us with adequate strength for the fight. "Be strong" is passive in the Greek. That indicates it is not something that we do to or for ourselves, but something that comes from outside of us. It is something that happens to us, not something that happens by us. "Be strengthened" would be a better way of capturing the meaning.

Paul has already told us in Ephesians about the power of God available to us. In Chapter 1 Paul prayed for the Ephesians that "the eyes of your heart may be enlightened, so that you may know what is the hope of His calling, what are the riches of the glory of His inheritance in the saints, and what is the surpassing *greatness of His power* toward us who believe." That is the same *"working of the strength of His might* which He brought about in Christ, when He raised Him from the dead and seated Him at His right hand in the heavenly places" (Ephesians 1:17-20ff).

Paul is telling us to be strengthened in the power of the One "who is *able to do* far more abundantly beyond all that we ask or think, according to *the power that works* within us" (Ephesians 3:20). That is the power that is described here.

192

We can and must trust that our adequacy and strength comes by the power of God. It is not in ourselves. It is in Christ. Everything necessary for the war has been given to us in Him. In ourselves, we are no match for the enemy. Once we rely upon our own strength for the battle, we're done. We cannot stand against the enemy in our own strength. He is smarter, stronger, and craftier than we are.

One of the subtle schemes of the enemy is to get us to try to be strong in ourselves. He wants us to think that we have some inherent strength and power to live the Christian life on our own. He wants us to think that we can stand apart from God's sustaining grace and the strength that Christ gives. Satan is delighted if we are strong in ourselves, for a misplaced trust is no trust at all. An ill-gotten strength is no strength at all. Satan does not fear those who think they are adequate in themselves for the task. If you think that your adequacy for the battle is in your spiritual giftedness, your firm resoluteness, your wisdom, your youth, your intelligence, your education, or your experiences, the enemy has you right where he wants you - in his crosshairs.

This self-reliant strength is the very thing I have described in the previous chapters. Those who think that their incantations, rote prayers, and repeated mantras are sufficient tools to take on the enemy of our souls are trusting in the wrong source of strength. They argue that the authority and power behind these "tools" is the Lord, but when someone employs unbiblical and extra-biblical tactics derived from witty conversations with demons, anecdotal evidences, and life experiences, they are, in fact, trusting in themselves and their own wisdom. They are relying upon carnal weapons that God has not promised to bless or empower.

Second, He has provided us with an adequate defense. Our adequate defense is the "full armor of God." This defense is useless unless we put it on.

The word translated "put on" is the word ἐνδύω (enduo) and it means "to envelop in, to hide in or to clothe with." It has the idea of dressing oneself with something. It is in the aorist tense which indicates a completed, once-for-all action. The protection which we have been given is never to be taken off. We never let our guard down.

Having once been clothed with this armor, we are never to find ourselves undressed.

Paul describes our "adequate defense" with the words "full armor." That was a word that was used to describe a heavily armed soldier. It literally means "all the weapons." We are to put on the full armament which God has graciously provided for us in Christ.

Paul would've been very familiar with the armor of a Roman soldier. By the time he wrote Ephesians, Paul had spent four years as a prisoner of the Roman Empire under constant supervision and guard.[1] Paul likens our defense to the armor of a Roman soldier.

Paul calls this the armor "of God." That is significant. The armor is not something which we provide or make. The armor is provided by God, for it comes from God. All the pieces of the armor listed in verses 14-17 refer to things provided by God to His people.

v. 14   loins girded with **truth** and breastplate of **righteousness**

v. 15   feet shod with the gospel of **peace**

v. 16   shield of **faith**

v. 17   helmet of **salvation** and the sword of the **Spirit** - the Word of God

All these are provided for us in salvation. They are not manufactured by us. Neither are they things which we contribute to our salvation. They are all part of the salvific package, given to us in Christ along with every other spiritual blessing in the heavenly places (Ephesians 1:3). If you are a believer in Christ, then you already have truth, righteousness, peace, faith, salvation, and the Holy Spirit. You are to put them on (appropriate them). You are to clothe yourself with them. These are your defense.

Our Adversary Is Satan

"So that you will be able to stand firm against the schemes of the devil. For our struggle is not against flesh and blood, but against

---

[1] Paul spent two years in Caesarea under Felix (Acts 24:27) and two years in Rome under house arrest (Acts 28:30).

the rulers, against the powers, against the world forces of this darkness, against the spiritual forces of wickedness in the heavenly places" (Ephesians 6:11b-12).

We are to take the full armor of God in order that we may be able to stand against the devil and his schemes. Our Commander in Chief has already done the reconnaissance of the enemy for us. He has issued a briefing describing our enemy, his territory, his manner of operation and his strength and tactics. This is revealed in Scripture, our sufficient source of information. We are given all that we need to know. So sufficient is the Scripture that Paul can say in 2 Corinthians 2:11 that we are "not ignorant of his [the devil] schemes."

We face a very real enemy. He is not a myth or a fairytale, but a real spirit-being with real power. He is the relentless enemy of the believer.

Charles Spurgeon wrote,

There is no believer in Christ, no follower of that which is true and lovely and of good repute, who will not find himself, at some season or other, attacked by this foul fiend and the legions enlisted in his service. Behold your adversary. Though you cannot see his face and detect his form, believe that such a foe withstands you. He is not a myth, nor a dream, nor superstitious imagination. He is as real a being as ourselves. Though a spirit, he has as much real power over hearts as we have over the hearts of others, nay in many more cases far more. This is no vision of the night, no phantom of a disordered brain. That wicked one is as sternly real this day as when Christ met him in deadly conflict in the wilderness of temptation.[2]

The danger he poses is a real one. Paul describes his tactics as "schemes." We get our English word "method" from the Greek word.[3] The only other time that that word is used in the New Testament is in Ephesians 4:14 where we are told to "no longer be

---

[2] Charles H. Spurgeon, *Spiritual Warfare in a Believer's Life* (Lynnwood: Emerald Books, 1993), 100.
[3] μεθοδεία (methodeia).

195

children, tossed here and there by waves and carried about by every wind of doctrine, by the trickery of men, by craftiness in deceitful scheming." The word refers to "a craft," or "a deceit." It was the word used which described a predator laying a trap, a deceitful scheme for its prey. The goal of Satan's schemes is our total destruction. As C. H. Spurgeon notes,

> Nothing short of the total destruction of a believer will ever satisfy our adversary. Satan would rend the believer in pieces, break his bones, and utterly destroy him if he could. Do not, therefore, indulge the thought that the main purpose of Satan is to make you miserable. Satan is pleased with that, but that is not his ultimate end. Sometimes he may even make you happy, for he has dainty poisons sweet to the taste that he administers to God's people. If he feels that our destruction can be more readily achieved by sweets than by bitters, he certainly would prefer that which would best effect his end.[4]

We can discern from Paul's words that Satan has a whole host of helpers at his disposal. These demon powers are described in verse 12 in four phrases that each begin with the word "against."

. . . against the rulers

. . . against the powers

. . . against the world forces of this darkness

. . . against the spiritual forces of wickedness in the heavenly places

Some deliverance ministry teachers have suggested that these four phrases describe the hierarchy of Satan. They suggest that "rulers" refers to the chief demons of Satan's kingdom with "powers" below them, then "forces of darkness," and, below them and last on the totem pole, the "spiritual forces of wickedness."

For instance, Mark Bubeck, demonstrating great imagination and poor exegesis, makes reference to Ephesians 6:12:

> These spirit beings are also very structured, organized and disciplined. We gain insight into this fact by the mention of

---

[4] Spurgeon, 107.

these foes who serve under Satan's control in Ephesians 6:12. The picture is one much like that which prevails in a military organization. At the top of America's military structure is our President, the Commander-In-Chief of all military forces. Under him are the commanding generals, the admirals, and all of the other officers on down to the lowly private.

This is the same kind of structure which is suggested here in Ephesians 6. Satan is the commander-in-chief of the forces of darkness. He is the supreme strategist, and under him is a highly organized system which is as disciplined to carry out Satan's wishes as he can make it.

The first level under Satan is a group of commanders called "principalities" or "princes." These powerful beings carry vast responsibility and power to guide the affairs of Satan. . . . The next level down in this organized structure are the "powers." These are probably more numerous and somewhat less independent and powerful than the princes. . . . The next level down in the organization of evil are the "rulers of darkness." These beings are more numerous; yet they are the real workhorses on the command level. Their counterparts in the Army might be the lieutenants and sergeants of our military forces. These rulers of darkness have directly under them a very fast final level of spirit beings called "spiritual wickedness" or "wicked spirits" in high places.[5]

This is not what Paul is getting at! Paul is giving us four phrases that describe the character and activity of our enemy, not the ranks

---

[5] Mark I. Bubeck, *The Adversary: The Christian Versus Demonic Activity* (Chicago: Moody Press, 1975), 72-73. Ephesians 6:12 does not teach or even suggest such a highly detailed hierarchy of power, ability, and command. Where does Bubeck get his information about what each level does and how many demons occupy each group? How does he know that "princes" "carry vast responsibility and power to guide the affairs of Satan"? How does he know that "rulers of darkness" are "more numerous" and "are the real workhorses" of Satan's activity? He seems to invent it out of his own mind! He certainly does not derive this from the text.

of his military. No doubt there are levels of authority and activity in Satan's kingdom, but this text does not describe that. These words describe the nature of demonic forces and their activities. They are "rulers" of darkness. They are spiritual "powers." They are worldwide forces which promote darkness. They are not physical forces but spiritual forces which work wickedness and reside in the heavenly places (spiritual realm). At the risk of sounding redundant, Paul is reminding us that our struggle is "not against flesh and blood."

It is important for us to remember that our real enemies are not physical. Will people oppose you? Certainly. Will people try to stop you from living your faith, witnessing, and doing the will of God? Certainly. Paul was more than familiar with human opposition. When he was in prison, Demas forsook him (2 Timothy 4:10). Alexander the Coppersmith did him much harm (2 Timothy 4:14). He fought with false teachers and Judaizers who plagued his steps and sought to undo his work. Some in the church of Corinth hated him, slandered him, lied about him, mocked him, and spread false reports about him. There were those who twisted his teaching and stole his converts. Some questioned his authority and mocked his physical appearance. There were those who persecuted him and worked for his execution. In fact, he wrote the book of Ephesians while awaiting trial before Nero, under house arrest, charged with false accusations.

Paul knew human opposition, yet he also knew that the real enemy was not "flesh and blood." The enemy behind all human opposition to the cause of Christ is the spiritual forces of wickedness which are at work in the heavenly places. Men and women are not our true enemies.

Your battle is not against the boss who won't let you leave your Bible on your desk. The enemy is not the school principal who won't allow your child to wear a Christian T-shirt. The enemy is not the humanist judge who rules that "under God" in the Pledge of Allegiance is unconstitutional. The enemy is not a political party, a candidate, a congressman, the unsaved spouse hostile to Christ, or a local elected official. The enemy is not the abortion provider, the homosexual activist, or the ACLU. These people are not the enemy - they are the mission field!

The real battle is with the rulers of darkness - with Satan and his fallen angels who control the thinking of the world, influence their behavior, and deceive them into thinking that those things are true, right, and good. Those that we often perceive as the enemy are those who need to "escape from the snare of the devil, having been held captive by him to do his will" (2 Timothy 2:26).

This information is not intended to terrorize us into fearful inactivity. We should not think that there is a demon under every rock and behind every tree. Such fearful preoccupation is neither healthy nor biblical. Though our enemy is real, crafty, and dangerous, we need not fear since the Lord has provided adequate strength and adequate defense. This is why we are to clothe ourselves with all that God has provided for our protection.

Our Approach Is to Stand

"Therefore, take up the full armor of God, so that you will be able to resist in the evil day, and having done everything, to stand firm. Stand firm . . . " (Ephesians 6:13-14a).

Paul encourages us to "take up the full armor of God." The description of the nature and work of Satan and his demons is sandwiched between these commands to "take up the full armor of God" (vv. 11 & 13).

So important is the armor of God that without it, we will be unable to "stand" or "resist." The only person able to stand against the schemes of the devil is a believer who appropriates all that Christ has provided. An unbeliever cannot stand. Unbelievers cannot and do not resist the devil, for they have no armor. Unbelievers cannot even put on this armor. They are dead in trespasses and sins, being children of wrath (Ephesians 2:1-3), and children of the devil (John 8:44). Unbelievers do not know the truth, they do not have the righteousness of Christ, they do not have peace with God, they do not have salvation, they have never exercised faith, and they do not have the Holy Spirit. These are all the parts of the armor. These are

199

the things provided to God's elect in salvation. An unbeliever has no part in them.

It is only Christians who have been delivered from the "evil day." Some have understood the reference to "evil day" to describe times or seasons of intense temptation, distress, or pointed satanic attack. They would suggest that there are certain seasons in which we are more intensely attacked than at others. However, Paul has already told us what the "evil day" is in Ephesians 5:16: "Making the most of your time, because the days are evil." Every day since Adam ate the forbidden fruit in the garden has been an evil day. Every day is filled with evil. Yesterday was an evil day. Today is an evil day. Tomorrow will be an evil day.

We are not only to be on guard at times of particular temptation, but every day. We are not only supposed to resist when we feel the most opposition, but at all times. The armor is not intended only for days of intense temptation, distress, or satanic attack. The armor is intended to be ours at all times, in all places - every day.

Paul says that "having done everything" we are to stand. What does he mean by "having done everything"? I believe he is referring to all of the imperative commands that he has given us from 4:1 to 6:9. Having accomplished all that God has given us to do, having walked the walk that we have been called to walk (4:1), having cast off the deeds of darkness (5:11), having made the most of every opportunity (5:15), having submitted to one another in the fear of Christ (5:18), we are to stand.

The Christian life is a life lived in heartfelt obedience to the commands of our Sovereign. We know that we have "put on the Lord Jesus Christ" (Romans 13:14) when we are walking in obedience to the commands of the Lord.

Notice how often Paul tells us we are to "stand." The idea of "standing" is a central theme of the passage. A quick read of the entire passage will show the repetition. Paul mentions the need to stand four times in Ephesians 6:

v. 11 ". . . so that you will be able to stand firm . . . "

v. 13 ". . . so that you will be able to resist[6] in the evil day. . ."

v. 13 ". . . having done everything, to stand firm."

v. 14 " Stand firm therefore, . . ."

This describes the posture with which we do battle. Spiritual warfare is described in terms of "standing." In passages which give instruction on dealing with the devil, we are told to stand. Both James and the Apostle Peter give the same instruction as Paul.

1 Peter 5:8–9: "Be of sober spirit, be on the alert. Your adversary, the devil, prowls around like a roaring lion, seeking someone to devour. But resist him, firm in your faith, knowing that the same experiences of suffering are being accomplished by your brethren who are in the world."

James 4:7: "Submit therefore to God. Resist the devil and he will flee from you."

Both James and Peter say we are to "resist." They use the same word that Paul uses in Ephesians 6 which is there translated "stand."[7]

Notice how different this approach is from the one I have been critiquing in previous chapters. We are not called to go crashing and smashing down the gates of hell, claiming dominion, winning back territory, exorcising demons, binding the devil, casting him down, away, or out, and ordering him to the pit of hell. Scripture does not teach us to develop a strategy of spiritual warfare based upon personal experience, anecdote, or conversations with demons. We are not to pursue a strategy that is marked by rebuking, binding, insulting, or arguing with Satan and his demons. We are not involved in a war for territory, but for truth.

Our warfare is not an offensive strategy intended to secure territory. We are to be on the offensive only in the sense that we attack false ideologies, preach the word, proclaim the gospel, and go into all the world to make disciples. In terms of our approach to the

---

[6] It is a form of the same word translated "stand" in the other verses.

[7] Ephesians 6:11 - ἵστημι (histemi - to stand); Ephesians 6:13 - ἀνθίστημι (anthistemi - to set one's self against); Ephesians 6:13 - ἵστημι (histemi - to stand); Ephesians 6:14 -ἵστημι (histemi - to stand); 1 Peter 5:8-9 - ἀνθίστημι (anthistemi- to set one's self against); James 4:7 - ἀνθίστημι (anthistemi - to set one's self against).

spiritual forces of wickedness, we are commanded to resist and stand in the truth.

All of the methods critiqued in this book have this one thing in common: they are either unbiblical or extra-biblical. The modern approach to spiritual warfare engages in practices to which we are not called and in which we are not instructed. We are called to stand. Any other approach is disobedience to our Commander-in-Chief.

The problem within the church is not that Christians don't know how to do exorcisms, break generational curses, bind Satan, or use prayer mantras to manipulate demons. The problem in modern evangelicalism is that Christians aren't standing. The church loses effectiveness when it compromises the truth. There can be no gain of territory when we are losing the truth battle. The vexing state of the church is due to the fact that it is spiritually anemic. Christians are compromising doctrine and morals in their daily lives. Men do not stand as the leaders and protectors of their homes. Men do not lead and serve in the church. Christians today are more interested in pandering to the world and aping the culture than they are in taking a hard stand for truth and doctrinal purity.

Evangelicalism has bought the postmodern lie that it is intolerant and unloving to condemn any lifestyle or doctrine. Christians are not interested in obedience. Churches are not interested in exercising church discipline. The commands of Scripture are seen as optional rather than binding. These and many more are the symptoms of a church that does not stand.

The visible church is not standing. It is losing the battle for truth. No unbiblical practice, and no combination of unbiblical practices, can remedy this present crisis. Unbiblical tactics cannot advance the kingdom of God. Christians are losing the spiritual battle because they refuse to stand.

Spiritual Warfare and Humility

It is quite noteworthy that in the context in which both Peter and James tell us to stand, they were discussing the subject of humility.

1 Peter 5:6: "You younger men, likewise, *be subject* to your elders; and all of you, clothe yourselves with *humility* toward one another,

for God is opposed to the proud, but gives grace to the *humble*. Therefore *humble* yourselves under the mighty hand of God, that He may exalt you at the proper time."[8] Immediately following this exhortation to humility, Peter warns us about our prowling adversary, and then says that we are to "resist him, firm in the faith" (5:8-9).

Likewise, James's instruction on resisting the devil is sandwiched between two exhortations to humility. Look at the entire context of the passage referenced earlier, James 4:6–10:

But He gives a greater grace. Therefore it says, "God is *opposed to the proud*, but gives grace to the *humble*." Submit therefore to God. Resist the devil and he will flee from you. Draw near to God and He will draw near to you. Cleanse your hands, you sinners; and purify your hearts, you double-minded. Be miserable and mourn and weep; let your laughter be turned into mourning and your joy to gloom. *Humble yourselves* in the presence of the Lord, and He will exalt you.[9]

Why do you suppose there is such an emphasis on humility when giving instruction on dealing with the devil?

Humility is the mark of those who are clothed in the armor of God. Those who have "put on the Lord Jesus Christ"[10] have appropriated the grace that is theirs in Christ. They are those who are obedient to the Lord. They know that their own strength is insufficient to stand against the wiles of the devil, and so they rely upon the strength which God supplies. They know that they, their authority, their abilities, their wisdom, their discernment, are all inadequate to the task of resisting so lethal and formidable a foe. They do not lean on their own understanding. They do not trust in their own strength. They are humble.

Only the humble are able to truly stand. God does not supply strength to the proud. God resists the proud. "The fear of the LORD

---

[8] Emphasis mine.
[9] Emphasis mine.
[10] Romans 13:14.

203

is to hate evil; Pride and arrogance and the evil way and the perverted mouth, I hate" (Proverbs 8:13). Those who are prideful set themselves up for a fall and for destruction as Proverbs 16:18 says, "Pride goes before destruction, and a haughty spirit before stumbling."

Such an encouragement to humility is desperately needed today, especially in modern "deliverance ministries." I don't believe that those who claim all of Christ's authority for themselves, the power to bind the devil, to break curses, to send demons to hell, to crush Satan, to rebuke demonic powers, and to cast out demons, can be described as humble. In fact, the approach taken by modern deliverance ministry "experts" toward Satan and his powers smacks of pride, not humility.

A Final Thought on Standing

Those who advocate an aggressive, Satan-stomping, demon-demolishing, hand-to-hand-battle-for-territory type of approach to spiritual warfare do not find their approach described or prescribed in Scripture. Instead, we are called to stand.

We are obligated to follow the instructions in Scripture. In those passages where our marching orders are given, the word is clear: stand. He has only given us one strategy. Our Lord has told us what He expects. The only effective method of spiritual warfare is to rely upon the Lord for strength, appropriate the grace we have been given, obey the command of our King, and stand firm in the gospel, in truth, and in His righteousness. Any other approach exposes us to the deceptions and power of the enemy. There is only one approach to spiritual warfare that Christ honors. There is only one method which secures the protection of our Sovereign. There is only one posture that reflects humility and unquestioning obedience to the Word of God. Stand. So, stand! It really is that simple.

15

The Protection for a Soldier

Finally, be strong in the Lord and in the strength of His might. Put on the full armor of God, so that you will be able to stand firm against the schemes of the devil. For our struggle is not against flesh and blood, but against the rulers, against the powers, against the world forces of this darkness, against the spiritual forces of wickedness in the heavenly places. Therefore, take up the full armor of God, so that you will be able to resist in the evil day, and having done everything, to stand firm. Stand firm therefore, having girded your loins with truth, and having put on the breastplate of righteousness, and having shod your feet with the preparation of the gospel of peace; in addition to all, taking up the shield of faith with which you will be able to extinguish all the flaming arrows of the evil one. And take the helmet of salvation, and the sword of the Spirit, which is the word of God (Ephesians 6:10–17).

To borrow words from the Apostle Paul, "Finally, my brethren," we come to the armor of God. The passage on the armor of God serves as a perfect conclusion to the book of Ephesians, and its positive instruction regarding spiritual warfare serves as a perfect conclusion to this book.

I used to entertain notions about the armor of God which are now embarrassing. When I first became a Christian, I was obsessed with making sure that I was not a victim of Satan and his deceptions. Unwittingly, my preoccupation with Satan and demons in an effort to *avoid* deception ended up deceiving me!

Ephesians 6:10-17 became very familiar to me as I studied it, heard it lectured on, and read material about how to appropriate the armor of God and avoid the temptations and attacks of the devil. I could recite that passage from memory, though my knowledge of the material in the other five chapters of Ephesians was woefully lacking.

As a new believer, I had a lot of wrong ideas about what spiritual warfare was and how it was waged. I knew that I had to "put on the full armor of God" and "take up the full armor of God" (Ephesians 6:11,13), but it was a mystery to me as to how exactly this was to be done. After all, it was "spiritual" armor. How do you "put on" or "take up" something that you cannot see or touch? If these are spiritual pieces, how do I spiritually pick them up and put them on? I thought that the armor was something that had to be "put on" every morning, or even several times a day. I even imagined it was something that was done in prayer as each piece of the armor was specifically named, prayed about, and appropriated.

Further, I had been taught that failure to put on these pieces left me a sitting duck before my mortal foe. I had learned that victory over sin and temptation was only possible for the one who put on the armor. I was terrified that I would not be immune to generational curses and sins. I wanted to be free from temptation, trials, and deception. I was convinced that these things would only be a reality if I was diligent to put on the armor. But again, HOW?

Spiritual warfare "experts" are quick to offer suggestions as to just how this should be done. Mark Bubeck, never one to miss an opportunity to offer a formulaic prayer for a given situation, suggests "a typical prayer one might use in putting on his armor."[1] The following are excerpts from this prayer:

Heavenly Father, I desire to be obedient by being strong in the Lord and the power of Your might. . . . I delight to take the armor You have provided and by faith to put it on as effective spiritual protection against the spiritual forces of darkness. . . . I confidently take the loin girdle of truth that

---

[1] Mark I. Bubeck, *The Adversary: The Christian Versus Demon Activity* (Chicago: Moody Press, 1975), 74-77.

You offer me. I take Him who is the truth as my strength and protection. I reject Satan's lies and deceiving ways to gain advantage against me . . . . I desire to believe only the truth, to live the truth, to speak the truth, and to know the truth. . . .

Thank You for the breastplate of righteousness which You offer me. I eagerly accept it and put it on as my protection. . . . I reject and repudiate all trust in my own righteousness which is as filthy rags. . . . I bring the righteousness of my Lord directly against all of Satan's workings against me. . . . I know that Satan must retreat from before the righteousness of God.[2]

In order to put on the sandals of peace, Bubeck instructs us to pray:

Thank You, Lord, for the sandals of peace You have provided. . . . I claim the peace with God which is mine through justification. I desire the peace of God which touches my emotions and feelings through prayer and sanctification. Thank You that as I walk in obedience to You that the God of peace promises to walk with me, that as the God of peace You are putting Satan under my feet. . . . Thank You that Satan cannot stand against Your peace.

This type of spiritual "putting on" of the armor of God is repeated as each piece of the armor is named, explained, and spiritually received in prayer. In order to have the salvation helmet one should pray, "I recognize that my mind is a particular target of Satan's deceiving ways. I take from You the helmet of salvation. I cover my mind, my thoughts, with Your salvation. . . . I helmet my head with Him [Christ]. . . ."

For the sword of the Spirit, which is the Word of God, Bubeck suggests praying:

---

[2] Ibid., 74-75.

With joy I take hold upon the sword of the Spirit, which is the Word of God. . . . Enable me to use Your Word not only to defend me from Satan, but also to claim its promises and to wield the sword strong against Satan to defeat him, to push him back, to take away from him ground he claims, and to win great victories for my God through Your Word. Thank You that Satan must retreat from Your Word applied against him.[3]

Bubeck teaches that the armor must be put on in this fashion by prayer each and every day, perhaps several times a day.[4] As a young believer, this is exactly how I thought the armor was to be appropriated. I thought that each piece of the armor needed to be put on through envisioning myself taking and applying each piece as I prayed over each individual one.

The antidote for this wrong view of the armor is a correct understanding of the *context* which is the entire book of Ephesians.

The Dangers of Divorcing Context

When this passage on the armor of God is considered apart from its larger context, we are left to our own subjective imagination as to how the armor is to be "taken up" or "put on." This was my problem early in my Christian life. I knew the pieces of the armor by heart, but I had no idea what it meant to "put on" these pieces. This subjective approach leads to all kinds of mystical, gnostic, superstitious approaches to the armor.

Typically, Ephesians 6:10-17 is divorced from its context and interpreted as if it stands alone. The passage is the conclusion to the book of Ephesians and should be viewed as such. In other words, the analogy of the armor should be interpreted as a summary, a conclusion to all that has been said in the previous five chapters. All the presentations on the armor of God that I had heard never treated the armor of God as the conclusion of the book. A little context goes a long way toward clearing up confusion.

---

[3] Ibid., 76.
[4] Ibid., 73, 76.

208

Each piece of the armor of God is developed at length through the whole book of Ephesians. Ephesians 6 is not the first place in Ephesians that we read of truth, righteousness, the gospel of peace, faith, salvation, or the Word of God. These are all themes that Paul has explained throughout the book. They meet in this final summary passage which serves as a conclusion to Ephesians.

Another result of divorcing this passage from its context is it tends to make more out of the analogy of the Roman armor than Paul may have intended. There is no doubt that the passage is an analogy. Paul likens these various provisions of salvation to the pieces of armor worn by a Roman soldier.

Knowing that, we must answer several interpretive questions. For instance, what is the point of the analogy? What did Paul intend for us to understand by his reference to this "armor"? Should we take the analogy as a whole or are we to understand the passage through the sum of its individual parts?

The point of the analogy is not its reference to the individual parts, but in understanding the armor as a whole. This is where we run into the danger of making more out of the analogy of the Roman soldier than Paul intended. Typically we see the armor treated as if it is a list of individual pieces, any one of which we may take up or not take up. For instance, here is how the "breastplate of righteousness" is typically taught.

A lot of ink is spilled in detailing what the breastplate was, what it looked like, and how it functioned. The breastplate of a Roman soldier was used to protect the vital organs. What are those vital organs? The heart and bowels. In Jewish thinking, the heart represented the seat of the mind and the will, and the bowels represent the seat of the emotions. Therefore God has provided something which protects our mind and emotions: righteousness. Then we start to ask the question, "How is it that righteousness guards my mind and emotions?" This is where teachers and commentators find the freedom to run astray with all kinds of suggestions and applications as to what Paul meant.

No one stops to ask the question, "Is the point of that reference to be found in the function of the breastplate, or is the point of that reference to be found in the meaning of "righteousness"? The point of the reference is to be found in the meaning of righteousness not in the function of the breastplate. After all, don't truth, peace, salvation, and the Word of God also serve to guard our will and emotions?

Paul does not tell us what he had in mind when he attaches truth with belt, righteousness with breastplate, and peace with feet. When each piece is considered and applied apart from the whole, the "armor of God" becomes a subjective exercise in creative thinking and wild imaginations restrained only by the whim and will of the interpreter rather than the text. There is a better and more textually-grounded way of approaching the armor.

"Belt" does not illustrate the purpose of "truth" in the life of a believer, nor does "breastplate" illustrate the function of "righteousness" in the life of a believer. The main point of the analogy is not in the function of the individual pieces at all. The point of the analogy is in the function of the whole. The point is not to be found in the clothing, but in the attributes that are mentioned: truth, righteousness, peace, faith, salvation, and the Word of God.

Twice in this passage, Paul refers to the "whole armor of God" (vv. 11, 13). So let's look at the armor as a whole.

What a Soldier Wore

Paul's readers would have been familiar with the armor of a Roman soldier. Though we do not want to make more of the analogy than is intended, we don't want to ignore it either. Let's take a look at what a Roman soldier wore.

Belt: The belt of a soldier was important. It might not seem like an essential piece of our attire today, but in the days of robes and loose tunics, the belt played a vital role. It was used to tie up the loose ends of the soldier's clothing. The tunic was a square piece of material with holes cut for the head and arms. Before battle, the loose ends of the tunic would be cinched up into the belt and tucked in so there would be nothing to hinder the movement of the soldier.

Breastplate: The breastplate was a single piece of hammered metal. It was worn in the front and protected the vital organs.

210

Shoes: A soldier needed to be able to protect his feet from all sorts of terrain. The sandals worn by Roman soldiers were very durable and often had bits of metal or nails embedded in the soles to give traction and stability on uncertain terrain.

Shield: There were two types of shields used in Paul's day. The first was a small, round shield about two feet in diameter used for close hand-to-hand combat. This shield was attached to the arm with leather straps.

The second type of shield is the type that Paul mentions here. These were larger and rectangular in shape. They were typically four to four-and-a-half feet tall and two to two-and-a-half feet wide. These shields were used in conjunction with one another. Soldiers would line up shoulder-to-shoulder, putting their shields together to form a wall difficult to penetrate. Archers would stand behind the advancing wall, shoot at any who would try to climb over, and fire arrows over the top at the enemy. The shields were often coated with leather. The leather-coated shields would be soaked with water before going into battle, since it was the common practice to dip the tips of arrows in pitch or some other thick, burnable substance and light them before firing. When the arrow hit a target, the burning pitch would splatter onto the things around it and set the target on fire. The wet leather of the shield would serve to quench these fiery arrows.

Helmet: This protected the head of the soldier.

Sword: Every soldier needed a sword as an offensive weapon.

When we take the armor as a whole, a couple of things stand out. First, we notice the totality of the protection that the armor provides. Everything is covered from head (helmet) to toe (shoes). In other words, there is no part where the Christian is lacking for protection. God has provided adequate defense for the believer. We are not lacking anything we need in order to deal with the enemy and his schemes. God has given us everything that is necessary for this life and for godliness (2 Peter 1:3). If the enemy manages to be successful in his attacks, it is not due to a lack of God's provision, but some lack in our application of that provision.

211

Second, we notice that there is no armor provided for the rear. A soldier in retreat was provided no protection. A soldier who stood his ground would find himself well guarded from the enemy's weapons. There simply is no protection for the one who does not stand.

The main point of the analogy rests in the totality of our protection. That is the significant point. God has so wrapped you in His provision that there is no excuse not to stand. So long as you stand, and do not give ground to the enemy, there is no way for Satan to penetrate God's protection.

Now let's take a look at those things which Paul says make up our protection.

Ephesian Themes

If you were tasked with identifying the major themes of the book of Ephesians, do you know what you would find? If you study the book of Ephesians from its first verse, and you highlight those themes which surface again and again, you would find there are six: truth, righteousness, peace, faith, salvation, and the work of the Spirit of God. Not coincidentally, these six themes correspond to the armor of Ephesians 6. In this passage, all of the major themes, which have been developed at one point or another throughout the book, come together into one package.

Truth: Truth is mentioned on six other occasions in Ephesians (1:13; 4:15, 21, 24, 25; 5:9). The important point here is not, "What does a belt tell us about truth?" but, "What does the rest of Ephesians tell us about truth?"

Truth is the content of doctrine which we have believed for salvation (1:13). Truth matures us and grows us up in all aspects into Christ who is the Head (4:15). We find that the truth is in Jesus (4:21). We are a new man created in the truth (4:24) and so we are to lay aside all falsehood and speak the truth with each other (4:25).

So as those who have been saved by the truth, matured by the truth, created in the truth, and sanctified by the truth, we are to walk in that truth and in the fruit of it (5:9). This is in obvious contrast to Satan who walks in falsehood as the father of lies (John 8:44).

212

Righteousness: There are two types of righteousness. First, there is imputed righteousness. When you became a Christian, Christ took your sin and gave you His righteousness. Righteousness was credited to your account. It is not a righteousness which you earned or merited. It is a righteousness not derived from the law, but given by Christ.[5]

Second, there is practical righteousness. This is the righteousness which we practice when we walk in the truth. We are able to live a righteous life because we have been given the righteousness of Christ. It is our imputed righteousness which makes our practical righteousness possible.

Paul says we are to put on righteousness like a breastplate. Once again the question is not, "What does a breastplate teach me about righteousness?" but, "What do I know about righteousness from the rest of Ephesians?"

I believe that it is the practical righteousness that Paul is describing here. The two other times that Paul has mentioned righteousness, it has been connected with our walk. In Ephesians 4:24 we are told to "put on the new self, which in the likeness of God has been created in righteousness and holiness of the truth." In Ephesians 5:9 Paul said we are to walk in light because "the fruit of the Light consists in all goodness and righteousness and truth." In both of those contexts, there is a contrast between the righteous life of an obedient believer and the unrighteous conduct of a disobedient believer, or even an unbeliever.

We are to clothe ourselves with righteous conduct. The righteousness of Christ which has been provided for us in salvation is not something we can put on. It is something given to us by God. God clothes us in His righteousness. Righteous conduct, on the other hand, is something that I can "put on." As long as we practice righteousness and put off the deeds of darkness, we are protected. When we begin to live or trifle in unrighteousness, we give Satan an avenue by which he can attack.

---

[5] Philippians 3:7-11.

213

Peace: In connection with feet, Paul speaks of the gospel of peace. Peace is also mentioned five other times in Ephesians (1:2; 2:14, 15, 17; 4:3). Once again, the point of the analogy is not what sandals or feet tell us about the gospel or its proclamation, but, "What does the rest of Ephesians tell us about peace?"

Peace is something which comes to us from God our Father and the Lord Jesus Christ (1:2). The fact that Paul mentions the "gospel of peace" tells us exactly what he has in mind. The longest treatment of that theme comes in Chapter 2 where Paul shows how the gospel brings peace. He was not speaking about a "peaceful feeling" or a "peace in our spirit." Paul has something very specific in mind. In Chapter 2, he tells us how the gospel has brought peace between two groups of humanity who were once estranged. There was once a division between Jews and Gentiles. That division was created by the "law of commandments contained in ordinances." The gospel has changed that.

But now in Christ Jesus you who formerly were far off [Gentiles] have been brought near by the blood of Christ. For He Himself is our peace, who made both groups into one and broke down the barrier of the dividing wall, by abolishing in His flesh the enmity, which is the Law of commandments contained in ordinances, so that in Himself He might make the two into one new man, thus establishing peace, and might reconcile them both in one body to God through the cross, by it having put to death the enmity. And He came and preached peace to you who were far away, and peace to those who were near; for through Him we both have our access in one Spirit to the Father. So then you are no longer strangers and aliens, but you are fellow citizens with the saints, and are of God's household, having been built on the foundation of the apostles and prophets, Christ Jesus Himself being the corner stone, in whom the whole building, being fitted together, is growing into a holy temple in the Lord, in whom you also are being built together into a dwelling of God in the Spirit (Ephesians 2:13–22).

The gospel we have believed for our salvation (1:13-14) is a gospel that brings peace between men. It reconciles men to God, and men to men. It makes those who were once enemies, brothers. In the context of Ephesians, it is a peace between Jew and Gentile.

Just as Christ is our truth and our righteousness, He is also our peace as well. That peace which we now enjoy with the people of God, is something provided by God in our salvation. It is part of our protection from the enemy.

Faith: Faith is mentioned several times in Ephesians (1:15; 2:8; 3:12, 17; 4:5, 13; 6:23). Just as we have appropriated the other provisions of God's salvation, so we are to make use of faith in protecting us from the enemy. The question is not, "What does a shield teach me about faith?" but, "What does the rest of Ephesians tell me about faith?"

Faith, namely faith in Christ, is that which saves us (1:15; 2:1-10). Faith is a gift from God to His elect (2:8). Faith also gives us a continual access to the Father through Christ in prayer (3:12). By that same faith which has saved us, we are united together into one Body, the Church (4:5, 13). Faith is also something which comes from God to His people (6:23).

Though the enemy may throw fiery darts at us, we are protected by this continual trust in God. The faith which a believer exercises for salvation and protection is the gift of God to His people. It is a supernatural faith which is the result of God's sovereign gift. Just as we are saved, so we walk, and so we stand in and by faith.

Salvation: Salvation is the theme of the entire epistle (1:13; 2:5, 8). The point of the analogy is not "What does a Roman helmet tell me about salvation?" but, "What does the rest of Ephesians tell me about salvation?"

Chapters 1-3 tell us what salvation is, how it comes to us, Who has secured it, and what it has done for us. Chapters 4-6 show us the practical effects of salvation in our daily lives.

In 1:13 we are told that it is "the message of truth, the gospel of your salvation" which we believe and through that belief are sealed by the Holy Spirit. This salvation has come to us entirely by grace (2:5, 8).

215

Spirit of God/Word of God: The work of the Spirit of God in bringing salvation to His elect, and in sanctifying them, is evident throughout Ephesians (1:13; 2:18, 22; 3:5, 16; 4:3, 4, 30; 5:18; 6:18). At the risk of being redundant, the point of the analogy is not, "What does a sword tell me about the Word of God or the work of the Spirit?" but, "What does the rest of Ephesians tell me about the work of the Holy Spirit?"

We are "sealed with the Holy Spirit of promise" (1:13). In the power of the Holy Spirit we have access to the Father (2:18), and by Him God dwells in His people (2:22). The Holy Spirit has revealed to His holy apostles and prophets the ministry of the gospel which in previous ages was not known to men (3:5). Thus, the Holy Spirit is the One active in the giving of revelation and also illumination (3:16). The Holy Spirit has created a unity in the Church which we are to preserve (4:3-4). We are given strength to obey the injunctions of Scripture as we are filled with the Holy Spirit and mutually submit to one another in the fear of Christ (5:18-21). We are also to pray in the power of the Holy Spirit (6:18).

In the context of the armor of God, the work of the Spirit is pictured in terms of how He uses the Word of God to protect, defend, and equip us for battle.

The Spirit of God uses the Word of God as a weapon against Satan. Jesus modeled this in His temptation in the wilderness (Matthew 4:1-11). When Satan tempted Jesus, He responded with, "It is written."

The Word of God is both an offensive weapon and a defensive weapon. Its offensive quality is described in Hebrews 4:12: "For the Word of God is living and active and sharper than any two-edged sword, and piercing as far as the division of soul and spirit, of both joints and marrow, and able to judge the thoughts and intentions of the heart." That is what the truth does in spiritual warfare.

When we view spiritual warfare as a battle for truth rather than territory, then we can see how the Word of God is to be used. 2 Corinthians 10:3-5 tells us that the essence of spiritual warfare is the tearing down of ideologies, and mental strongholds in which unbelievers take refuge. Spiritual warfare is a truth war, not a territory war.

God's Word is truth, and by the proclamation of truth in the gospel and the Word of God, Satan's captives are set free from their mental strongholds. In the confrontation and conflict of delivering man from the kingdom of darkness, the only thing we have to use is the Word of God. We use it offensively in the sense that we preach it, teach it, stand for it, and confront people with its truth claims. We do this, trusting the Word of God will work in the hearts, lives, and minds of people to bring them to a knowledge of the truth so that they may be delivered from the snare of the devil (2 Timothy 2:25-26).

There is also a defensive use for the Word of God. When the enemy attacks, we always go back to Scripture. When we are tempted to doubt, we go to the Word. When we are tempted to worry, we go to the Word. When Satan brings discouragement, we go to the Word. When Satan brings depression, we find the answer in the Word. When the devil confronts us with error, we go to the Word of Truth. We always respond with the particular truth of Scripture which pertains to the temptation or attack. We can bank our lives upon that which is written by the Spirit of God.

C.H. Spurgeon wrote,

Let us fight Satan always with an "It is written," for no weapon will ever fight the archenemy as well as Holy Scripture. Attempts to fight Satan with a wooden sword of reason, and he will easily overcome you. But use the blade of God's Word, by which he has been wounded many times, and you will speedily overcome him. . . . "It is written." Stand upon it, and if the devil were 50 devils in one, he would not overcome you. On the other hand, if you leave "It is written," Satan knows more about reasoning than you do. He is far older, has studied mankind very thoroughly and knows all our weak points. Therefore, the contest will be an unequal one. Do not argue with him but wave in his face the banner of God's Word. Satan cannot endure the infallible truth, for it is the death to the falsehood of which he is the father.[6]

The Word of God must be something we study, love, read, memorize, and honor. To abandon the Word of God is to abandon the battle itself. Spiritual warfare is a truth war. The Word of God is truth. To put the Word on a shelf and refuse to use it, or to use another weapon in its place is to forfeit the entire battle.

Spurgeon said,

If you would successfully wrestle with Satan, make the Holy Scriptures your daily commune. Out of the sacred Word continually draw your armor and ammunition. Lay hold upon the glorious doctrines of God's Word; make them your daily meat and drink. So shall you be strong to resist the devil, and you shall be joyful in discovering that he will flee from you.[7]

What We Learn from the Armor

The armor (protection) God has provided is nothing less than Jesus Christ Himself. He is truth. He is our righteousness. He is our peace. He is the Author and Finisher of our faith. He is our salvation and the Captain of it. He is the living Word of God. To don this protection is to "put on the Lord Jesus Christ, and make no provision for the flesh in regard to its lusts" (Romans 13:14). Christ is our shield and our armor. He is our protection from Satan.

All that God has graciously provided for us in salvation (Ephesians 1-3) is to be lived out and appropriated in our daily lives (Ephesians 4-6). Spiritual protection results from walking in, working out, and living the salvation with which God has blessed us.

To be disobedient to God is to forfeit that protection and to yield to the enemy. Disobedience is a failure to stand in Christ. The degree to which we neglect any element of our walk is the degree to which we are vulnerable to the attacks of the enemy. The posture of the

---

[6] Charles Spurgeon, *Spiritual Warfare In A Believer's Life* (Lynnwood: Emerald Books, 1993), 37, 78.

[7] Ibid., 37.

soldier is to stand. The provision of protection for the soldier is our Savior.

The armor of God is the conclusion to the book of Ephesians. Paul is simply bringing all that he has said to a conclusion: Live out this great salvation. Walk in it. When you stand in Christ, you are protected from the wiles of the devil. There is nothing to fear for the one who is in Christ Jesus. The person who has been given salvation and makes their calling and election sure by walking in that salvation has nothing to fear from the enemy of their soul. They are protected because they are in Christ.

To "put on" or "take up" the whole armor of God *is to practically live out the graces of salvation which have been provided in Christ by God's rich blessings*. It is not something we mystically appropriate through a ritualistic prayer mantra. It is not something we speak into reality by positive confession. It is not a list of individual pieces which are "taken off" or "put on daily." It is the protection provided by being in God's Beloved Son. In Him we stand. We are safe from Satan so long as we walk in Him.

So stand in Him by *"walking in a manner worthy of the calling with which you have been called"* (Eph. 4:1). That is your protection.

16

Conclusion: A Final Appeal

What were you expecting when you purchased this book? Were you expecting a manual on spiritual warfare? Were you expecting a "how to" guide for hand-to-hand combat with demons? Were you hoping to find some formulaic prayers for defeating Satan, binding demons, and liberating loved ones? If so, then I am certain that by now you have one of two reactions.

First, you are really, REALLY mad at me. You might feel as if I have attacked your favorite teacher, undermined your experience, and questioned your discernment. If you are in this camp, then I want to thank you for reading all the way to the end. You could have stopped reading a long, long time ago.

Please understand that I feel your pain. I don't mean that condescendingly or as just a meaningless gesture. I *truly* understand your pain. As you may have picked up at various points in this book, there was a time when I believed, practiced, and embraced nearly every view on spiritual warfare that I have here critiqued. Through a growing understanding of the sufficiency of Scripture and the loving challenges of some friends, I was forced to evaluate these practices and then eventually to abandon them. I know from experience that it is not easy to jettison beliefs and traditions and to question experiences, especially those in which we are emotionally invested.

I am fine with a reader being mad at me. I only ask one thing: test what I have said to see if it is biblical. Test your own beliefs and presuppositions in the same way. I am not the final authority on these practices. Scripture is. So don't just test what I have written, test the writings of Anderson, Bubeck, White and the rest with the same standard.

Are they accurately handling the Word of Truth? Are their practices firmly rooted in sound doctrine and clearly spelled out in Scripture or are their teachings based on experience and the testimony of demons? Are these things taught and modeled in Scripture? Are these things commanded?

My appeal to you is this: go to the Word. Test all things and hold fast to that which is true (1 Thessalonians 5:21).

If you are not fuming mad at me, then you may be in a second camp: you feel a sense of liberation and freedom. You have come to understand that you don't have to live in fear. You don't have to recite mantras and prayer formulas. You don't have to worry that you may have unwittingly picked up a demon or a demonic influence. You don't have to battle curses, research territorial spirits, and ceremonially cleanse your environment in order to live a fruitful and productive Christian life.

You have come to firmly appreciate the death of Christ and what that has meant for you. You see now your complete deliverance from Satan and His kingdom. You fully appreciate the atonement of Christ and the redemption it has secured. Suddenly you realize that spiritual warfare is not as complicated and mystical as some have made it out to be. Things are so much simpler now. The clouds of confusion have vanished. You have been set free not only from Satan and his kingdom, but from a burdensome and unbiblical view of demons and spiritual warfare.

I feel your joy!

My appeal to you is this: go to the Word. Test all things and hold fast to that which is true (1 Thessalonians 5:21).

It is to the Word of Truth that we must run! It is sufficient. It is infallible. It is inerrant. It is God's Holy Word.

The present confusion and unbiblical practices of the spiritual warfare/deliverance ministry movement is nothing more than another sad manifestation of the modern church's lack of belief in the sufficiency of God's Word. It is my prayer that God will use the truth of His Word to expose error and bring down every false ideology

222

raised up against the knowledge of God - even the false ideology of the spiritual warfare movement.

About the Author

Jim Osman was born in May of 1972 and has lived in Sandpoint since he was three years old. He graduated from Sandpoint High School in 1990. Jim came to know Christ through the ministry of Cocolalla Lake Bible Camp in the summer of 1987. Kootenai Community Church has always been his home church, attending Sunday School, Vacation Bible School and Youth Group.

After graduating from High School, Jim attended Millar College of the Bible in Pambrun, Saskatchewan. It was at Bible College that Jim met his wife-to-be, Diedre, who was also enrolled as a student. Jim graduated with a three year diploma in April of 1993 and married Diedre in August of that same year. He returned to Millar to further his education in September of 1994 and graduated from the Fourth Year Internship Program with a Bachelor of Arts in Strategic Ministries in April of 1995. He was inducted into the Honor Society of the Association of Canadian Bible Colleges and appointed a member of Pi Alpha Mu.

Jim and Diedre returned to Sandpoint where Jim began working in construction as a roofer until he was asked to take over as the preaching elder of Kootenai Community Church in December of 1996. Now he counts it his greatest privilege to be involved in ministering in the church that ministered to him for so many years.

Jim loves to be outdoors, whether it is camping, hunting, or working in his garden. He enjoys bike riding and watching football, especially his favorite team, the San Francisco 49ers, for whom he has cheered since childhood. Jim and Diedre have four children: Taryn, Shepley, Ayden and Liam. They are all 49er fans!

You can contact Jim through Kootenai Community Church (http://www.kootenaichurch.org) or by writing to him at jimcosman@truthorterritory.com.

225